The New Review Economy

This book examines third-party review sites (TPRS) and the intersection of the review economy and neoliberal public relations, in order to understand how users and organizations engage the twenty-first-century global review economy.

The author applies communication and digital media theories to evaluate contemporary case studies that challenge TPRS and control over digital reputation. Chapters analyze famous cases such as the Texas photographer who sued her clients for negative reviews and activists using Yelp to protest the hunt of "Cecil the Lion," to illustrate the complicated yet important role of TPRS in the review economy. Theories such as neoliberal public relations, digital dialogic communication, and cultural intermediaries help explain the impact of reviews and how to apply lessons learned from infamous cases.

This nuanced and up-to-date exploration of the contemporary review economy will offer insights and best practice for academic researchers and upper-level undergraduate students in public relations, digital media, or strategic communication programs.

Alison N. Novak is an assistant professor at Rowan University in the Department of Public Relations & Advertising. Her work explores the intersections of digital media, public engagement, and policy. She is the co-author of *Network Neutrality and Digital Dialogic Communication*. Her work is featured on *BBC Radio*, *Wired Magazine*, and *The Huff Post*.

Routledge Focus on Public Relations

The New Review Economy

Third-Party Review Sites, Reputation, and Neo-Liberal Public Relations in the Digital Age

Alison N. Novak

Routledge
Taylor & Francis Group

NEW YORK AND LONDON

First published 2021
by Routledge
52 Vanderbilt Avenue, New York, NY 10017

and by Routledge
2 Park Square, Milton Park, Abingdon, Oxon OX14 4RN

Routledge is an imprint of the Taylor & Francis Group, an informa business

© 2021 Taylor & Francis

The right of Alison N. Novak to be identified as author of this work
has been asserted by her in accordance with sections 77 and 78 of the
Copyright, Designs and Patents Act 1988.

Library of Congress Cataloging-in-Publication Data
A catalog record for this title has been requested

ISBN: 9780367567071 (hbk)
ISBN: 9781003099437 (ebk)

Typeset in Times New Roman
by Newgen Publishing UK

Contents

Tables

Acknowledgments

This book would not be written without the support of my family, especially my parents, Michael and Denise Novak. I am grateful for their encouragement and support throughout the writing process.

I thank my mentors and colleagues at Rowan University and Drexel University, particularly my advisor Ernie Hakanen, for their help and guidance. Julie Richmond's contributions to Chapter 3 helped shape my early interest in third-party review sites. Earlier studies with Melinda Sebastian demonstrated why third-party review sites mattered in issues of advocacy and social movements. Portions of this project were presented at the National Communication Association Annual Convention and International Communication Association Annual Conference. I appreciate the effort of reviewers and conference participants, which strengthened this manuscript. Similarly, I thank the editorial team at Routledge for their hard work.

Finally, I thank my husband Greg who is one of the last subscribers to *Consumer Reports* and who deeply believes that our review culture makes the world a better place.

Introduction

In July 1936, a nonprofit group called *Consumer Reports*, opened its doors with a unique mission to "equip consumers with the 'knowledge they need to make better and more informed choices.'"[1] Over the course of the next eighty years, the group reviewed millions of products ranging from automobiles to vacuum cleaners to credit cards.[2] Publishing its findings in monthly magazines, *Consumer Reports* quickly became one of the most trusted sources for product insight featuring "editorial independence" and objectivity in its reviews.[3] Critical findings from *Consumer Reports* influenced both customer purchasing decisions as well as policy changes and federal investigations, including car-seat safety, hospital-borne illness rates, and computer virus susceptibility.[4] One mechanism for *Consumer Reports'* success was its "no commercial use" framework, which requested organizations not use reviews in advertising or marketing materials: "consumers should enjoy the full context of our information and not hear about our ratings and reports through the language of salesmanship."[5] In short, *Consumer Reports* sought to take power away from advertisers and return decision-making and product reputation to the hands of trained professional reviewers. In parallel with the growing distrust in the advertising and public relations industry throughout the twentieth century, *Consumer Reports* flourished. In return, brand managers scrambled to find ways to measure, evaluate, and respond to the beginnings of what is now known as the review economy.

The review economy is hallmarked by growing public trust and interest in product and organizational reviews. Whereas advertisers and public relations practitioners historically controlled organizational or product reputation, publications like *Consumer Reports* now held power over public perception. Although other forces such as news media, word-of-mouth, and competitor publicity could change public perception of a product, the growing trust in publications like *Consumer*

Reports meant that product or organizational success was now (at least somewhat) dependent on reviews.

Despite the historical success of *Consumer Reports*, recent research from *The Atlantic* argues that interest in the magazine is at its lowest point, and its function of reviewing is all-but replaced by the growing power of consumer-generated reviews such as those found on sites such as Yelp, Google Reviews, and myriad other platforms.[6] In short, a new era of review platforms was born, referred to as third-party review sites (TPRS). In just one decade, TPRS replaced *Consumer Reports* as the public's go-to source of reviews before making a purchasing decision. By 2019, a Nielsen study confirmed that 97 percent of people bought from local businesses they discovered or evaluated on Yelp. The study also noted that people trusted Yelp reviews in equal measure to those of *Consumer Reports* but found Yelp's online platform easier to navigate and appreciated the site's focus on local organizations. Survey respondents also liked the Yelp model, which allowed real customers to provide reviews, rather than objective reviews from paid professionals.[7]

With booming interest and trust in TPRS, Yelp faced competition from Google Reviews, which purchased Deja.com and Epinions, two of the earliest websites for consumers to post product reviews.[8] As public interest in *Consumer Reports* lagged, organizations now struggled to manage public feedback and reputation on sites like Yelp and Google Reviews. With the emergence of other digital spaces for online reviews, such as social media or owned-content review spaces (i.e. the customer comments section that appears after a product description on almost all online retailer webpages), organizations attempted to reconcile reviews as an important part of the twenty-first-century marketing and promotions mix.

TPRS are critical to managing the relationship between organizations and the public. As noted by *Forbes*, TPRS can make or break a company because of the vast amount of attention and trust given to public feedback: Yelp "harness[ed] shifts in consumer behavior to create the best marketing channel of all time for local businesses."[9] With over 142 million user visits each month, TPRS like Yelp have an incredible amount of power in the success of an organization. As a result, organizations learned to harness the power of TPRS through the integration of neoliberal public relations practices and dialogic communication. This book seeks to provide a comprehensive overview of TPRS and the theoretical and functional models of neoliberal public relations in the contemporary promotions mix. It provides a comprehensive overview of TPRS and how these sites use public labor to build both a digital reputation and cultivate engagement.

Third-Party Review Sites and the Review Economy

TPRS surged into popularity in the early 2000s as consumers looked for ways to finalize purchase or service decisions based upon credible consumer insight.[10] Zhou and Duan argued that TPRS were viewed by customers as more credible, accurate, and trustworthy because of the feedback mechanism that exists when consumers react to recent service or purchase experiences.[11] Customers identified TPRS as a site for digital feedback that could better inform future decisions. According to Zhou and Duan, the feedback mechanism emerged from social media culture, where users found that providing feedback and reflection on recent experiences was socially supported and part of the growing digital economy.[12] For scholars, the feedback mechanism motivates users to articulate, categorize, and rate purchases, service interactions, and social experiences using the affordances or abilities of social media and digital communication.[13] Yelp capitalized on the public's newfound adoption of the digital feedback mechanism by providing an online space where users could organize and share their reflections.[14]

Although TPRS are arguably the most well-known places to seek information and see the feedback mechanism, other types of publications, sites, and platforms similarly feature product or business reviews. These can be divided into five categories (see Table 0.1). First, objective, non-profit review platforms (although few) include *Consumer Reports* magazine. Publications like *Consumer Reports* are hallmarked by their non-profit origins that allow industry experts and trained professionals to make objective reviews without concerns over advertising revenues or profits. Today, in addition to physical magazines, objective, non-profit review publications also feature digital content, such as member-only access to magazine archives, and paywall articles posted to their websites. This type can also include organizations like the Better Business Bureau (BBB), a public–government partnership that monitors consumer referrals regarding unethical or problematic business practices. Members of the public can post reviews to the BBB's website which can motivate BBB investigations and legal actions.

Second, TPRS are websites and platforms completely dedicated to featuring reviews from members of the public. Unlike objective, non-profit review publications, TPRS allow nearly all individuals to post reviews based on consumer experiences such as recent purchases or organizational engagement. While Yelp is the most frequently visited of the TPRS, industry-specific sites also boast a loyal following. Students and professors are likely familiar with RateMyProfessor.com, an online

Table 0.1 Types of Review Spaces

Type	Objective, non-profit review platforms	TPRS	Social media	Owned review spaces	Non-owned review spaces
Examples	Consumer Reports, Better Business Bureau	Yelp, Google Reviews, Goodreads, RateMyProfessors, Glassdoor, FourSquare	Facebook, Twitter, LinkedIn	Bed, Bath & Beyond, Sephora, Home Depot	Amazon, TripAdvisor, Angie's List, OpenTable
Who reviews?	Trained industry experts	Public, current/past customers	Public, current/past customers	Public, current/past customers	Public, current/past customers
Can the organization modify the review?	No	No, but organizations can respond to posts if they are registered with the site	No, but organizations can appeal to the platform to edit or modify reviews that break content standards	Yes	No, but organizations can respond to customers and appeal to the platform to edit or modify reviews that break content standards

site that encourages students to post reviews of professors and classes for prospective students.

Third, social media platforms such as Facebook allow users to post reviews directly to organization pages. These reviews are structurally encouraged, giving organizations a specific space to solicit feedback from the public. Alternatively, social media platforms like Twitter allow users to organically mention or tag an organization in a post, allowing users to post feedback and ask questions. Other forms of reviews include "recommendations" on LinkedIn, which require user approval before they appear on an individual's profile.

Fourth, owned content reviews refer to customer feedback that appear on an organization's website. This semi-controlled space is located within the organization's website, therefore giving the organization the ability to delete or modify posts from consumers. Commonly, customer feedback is found below product descriptions or in a separate space such as a message board on the websites.

Finally, non-owned content reviews appear on websites that feature products, service, or profiles of a company, but are not owned by the organization. For example, Amazon boasts billions of products from millions of organizations. Each product page includes a section of "customer reviews" featuring a numerical star-system and open-ended comments. Customers can also post images of the products. Many of these product pages are created directly by the organization, but others are created directly by Amazon wholesalers. Either way, because the organization does not own the Amazon page, there are limited opportunities for an organization to challenge or modify negative reviews.

Lee and Blum note that TPRS, such as Yelp, gained popularity not only because of consumer use, but also because of perceived value to organizations.[15] The feedback provided within these spaces appealed to managers, owners, and public relations practitioners because of its relative honesty, detail, and low cost. Prior to the popularity of TPRS, it could take months to research and study customer satisfaction, often exclusively deriving from customer satisfaction surveys or mailed letters. TPRS sped-up review time, thus providing instantaneous and detailed insights into consumer behavior. While some organizations attempted to hide or minimize negative responses, Novak notes that most companies accepted the information and reviews as value to their business models.[16]

Although early scholarship on TPRS questioned the accuracy and honesty of the feedback left on sites such as Yelp and Google Reviews, recent research argues that most reviewers are likely to leave honest depictions of purchase and service experiences.[17] Most TPRS reviewers are also information seekers on the site, thus contributing to their motivation to provide accurate and honest feedback.[18] Yelp users argue that providing false information just to promote or damage a brand's reputation hinders the public's ability to make informed decisions.[19] Although there are many examples of organizations buying reviews or scrubbing (paying sites to remove or hide bad reviews), recent controversies on the sites have produced more oversight by the managing organizations to authenticate reviews and ensure accuracy.[20] For example, Yelp began flagging and eventually banning reviews by users who were known to offer pay-for-review services. The push for Yelp managers to intervene in corporate sabotaging instances (such as when an organization posts negative reviews of competitors) is driven by customer demands for honesty and accuracy on the site.[21]

Sperber argues that Yelp and other TPRS are part of a new phase of capitalism called the review economy.[22] While organization reputation was previously built on traditional advertising and public relations efforts, popularity now rests on public satisfaction and feedback.[23] Kuehn argues that throughout the 1970s, 1980s, and 1990s, the public grew increasingly dissatisfied and frustrated by marketing efforts that selectively hid and divulged information that only served to promote the brand.[24] Customers yearned for other, more credible ways of information-seeking prior to making a purchase; thus, the development of review publications.[25] Even in the earliest days of the Internet, users were already posting feedback and reflections on recent experiences in chatrooms and on wikis.[26] As the Internet gained more structure and increased popularity, sites like Yelp developed to provide organization to these reviews.[27]

Kuehn argues the review economy emerging from this feedback mechanism had ties to neoliberal labor and digital citizenship.[28] TPRS provide users a space to "take back" reputational control from the traditional advertising, public relations, and marketing efforts of an organization. The sites satisfy the frustrations that emerged in the 1970s to 1990s and provide a set of actions that consumers can take to insert themselves into the reputation-building process. According to Cockayne, users see themselves as part of a larger neoliberal system where the public works together to build a truthful reflection of public opinion of an organization or brand.[29] Here, consumers possess the power to alter public opinion and shape reputation.[30] Further, consumers feel compelled to participate in this process because of the neoliberal cultural context. Here, consumer experience is considered a collective responsibility of the public. This responsibility motivates individuals to post reflections and feedback that might better inform the actions of future customers.[31] This is particularly true of users who consult TPRS before making purchase decisions, thus benefiting from the work of other users.

TPRS and Neoliberal Public Relations

In his book, *Neo-PR*, Caldiero argues that public relations practitioners must increase the use of neoliberal labor.[32] The growth of public attention in the online environment provides numerous challenges to public relations practitioners hoping to direct and shape what users are (and are not) exposed to. Krinsky argues that, rather than reject this challenge or double-down on controlling online messaging, practitioners should take advantage of neoliberal labor available to digitally savvy online organizations.[33] This neoliberal public relations effort rests on organizations recognizing the value of digital communication and feedback that takes place on TPRS.[34] Rather than strive for traditional consistent messaging controlled by the organization and disseminated through select media, neoliberal labor relations suggest that the public is responsible for organizational reputation through the development of collective narratives or discourses surrounding a brand.[35] While an organization can (and should) respond to reviews and messages posted on TPRS, the public takes on the responsibility or labor of producing and disseminating information about the organization or brand.[36]

As discussed in the previous section, there are both benefits and concerns with giving more reputational control to the public.[37] However, most scholars credit the advantages of neoliberal public relations with the appointment of labor to users.[38] In addition to gaining third-party credibility through reviews and messaging, reviewers take on laborious tasks that were previously strictly restricted to public relations professionals.[39] While practitioners now must monitor these reviews for opportunities to respond or re-direct online discourse, the multitude of views expressed within TPRS offers more diversity in perspective than previously obtained through an individual practitioner.[40] Caldiero argues that many brands have only one practitioner or a small team working to regulate messaging in a digital space.[41] This means that messages are developed from one or two managerial points-of-view, rather than indicative of public trends or opinion.[42] According to Savini, even the most carefully crafted strategic messages are interpreted through the practitioners' lens and are thus removed from the positions of the public sphere.[43] Neoliberal labor, such as what occurs on TPRS, removes this barrier to "authentic messaging" and allows the public to develop its own discourse(s).[44] Scholars refer to this type of brand positioning as "quasi-upward communication," meaning public relations and management efforts take their cue from public feedback and messaging.[45] While it is not truly upward communication because users intend their reviews for other public readers, not top management, the information derived from these reviews by management does indicate its potential power in communication efforts.[46] For example, organizations now routinely use information, quotes, and opinions derived from TPRS and integrate them into new campaigns.[47] For example, healthcare service organizations use consumer reviews to improve doctor–patient relationships; politicians use reviews to revise policy decisions and initiatives; and educators use reviews to assess quality of instruction and teacher–student professionalism.[48] In short, organizations from a cross-section of industries take advantage of the reviews generated by users to craft communication campaigns, revise policies, and set future strategic goals.[49]

While most scholars praise the potential of neoliberal labor in digital spaces, some warn that the public may not openly accept or appreciate blatant campaigning or use of their reviews for organizational gain.[50] These reviews, posted on TPRS, are intended for other users so that they might gain insight into consumer experiences before making purchase decisions – not for organizational use or direct profit.[51] Mirftab argues that while users expect that organizations pay attention to their reviews, reviewers also lament aggressive responses or the use of their labor without compensation.[52] For Mirftab, and Aaron Richmond and Garmany, these two contrary ideas held by users about how their reviews should be integrated into organizational action, demonstrate the great challenge of neoliberal labor in brand management practices.[53] Organizations must both react and respond to user reviews but do so in a non-exploitative and respectful way that does not take advantage of the labor.[54]

TPRS' Impact and Importance

Examining the impact of TPRS is critical to understanding why these sites emerged as an important area of the twenty-first-century marketing and promotions mix. TPRS matter and hold a tremendous impact on the success of organizations around the world. According to Yelp, nearly 142 million unique users visit its platform each month to decide where to go to lunch; select a home repair person; register for wedding gifts; hire a tax professional; and virtually any other consumer decision.

Beyond the sheer number of people who turn to TPRS to make decisions, nearly 72 percent of visitors say that reading positive or negative reviews impacts their decisions at least once a week.[55] Positive reviews on Google Reviews drive both digital traffic to organizations' websites and are correlated with net increases in profits.[56] In short, organizations benefit from a positive presence on TPRS.

However, in addition to the increase in attention generated by TPRS, organizations benefit from the feedback provided. Rather than hiring a consulting firm to survey or host focus groups for suggestions, TPRS provide organizations with free feedback on organizational practices and policies. Of organizations who listened to customer feedback and adjusted policies and practices accordingly, 93 percent saw improved reviews on TPRS and 54 percent saw increases in profit.[57]

TPRS are not just considered important by organizations and users, scholars and journalists have reflected on the growing review economy and its ability to change promotions and marketing practices. *The Washington Post* reflects, "Having a good online reputation is important for everyone, but keeping up appearances on rating sites is particularly crucial for businesses in the Internet age."[58] *Forbes* adds, "The consumer decision making process is evolving. At the end of the day, consistent and recent reviews can impact a business's bottom line."[59] Further, scholarly findings demonstrate similar conclusions – TPRS are an important part of twenty-first-century organizational success. An article from the *Harvard Business Review* notes, "a one-star increase in Yelp rating leads to a 5–9 percent increase in revenue."[60] Sussman et al. reflect that more studies on TPRS like Yelp are critical to understanding how consumers make purchasing decisions as well as how the review economy continues to shape the culture.[61] With the growing demand for scholarly attention, this book attempts to address TPRS as a global force in the review economy.

Chapter Overviews

With the emergence of the review economy and the embrace of neoliberal public relations on TPRS, the power of reviews and their potential impact on organizational success grows. As journalists, scholars, and practitioners argue, TPRS are a key part of the twenty-first-century marketing and promotions mix, and understanding these sites is important for organizations. The remainder of this book examines TPRS from the perspective of users, organizations, elite reviewers, and advocates. The goal remains to provide a comprehensive overview of the power of TPRS, the contemporary challenges facing the review economy, and best practices for scholars and practitioners who engage with these sites.

The coming chapters highlight three important considerations for those engaging with TPRS and the review economy. First, case studies from TPRS can aid our understanding of what organizations and users should (and should not) do in the review economy. Second, neoliberal labor has replaced many of the traditional public relations and advertising practices, thus creating challenges for individuals charged with studying and protecting brand reputation. And, third, as TPRS continue to evolve, users will find unique ways to co-opt these spaces for non-traditional practices such as policy advocacy.

The book begins with an overview of these sites, how they have grown to popularity, and an analysis of how the design of TPRS' platforms impact user behavior. Chapter 1 introduces the evolution of TPRS and a synopsis of the conglomeration that occurred over the past ten years within the field. Chapter 2 then considers who posts to TPRS and how those posts impact other consumers. Using data from two international surveys of TPRS users, the chapter examines how differences in the demographics of reviewers and readers may contribute to falsities in online reviews. Chapter 3 identifies an important subset of TPRS contributors: super-reviewers. Participants in programs like the Yelp Elite Squad (YES) are prioritized by both the TPRS and organizations, and their reviews appear first on organizational pages. The chapter provides findings from interviews with international members of YES to understand how the group sees itself as a part of neoliberal public relations, the review economy, or the twenty-first-century promotions mix. Chapter 4 examines how organizations respond or react to reviews on TPRS, including a popular, unethical practice: scrubbing. The chapter looks at what happens when negative reviews are "scrubbed" away from an online profile after an organization pays a fee to the TPRS. Chapter 5 examines other organizational responses, including the legal steps that organizations take to combat negative or false reviews. The chapter addresses a key question: Can you be sued for a negative review? Next, Chapter 6 looks at how advocates have co-opted TPRS to promote policy changes or influence public opinion. Chapter 7 provides a series of best practices for users, organizations, and scholars who engage TPRS and the review economy. Finally, the book concludes with a reflection on how TPRS may evolve in the coming years. The conclusion pays attention to new TPRS and their implications for the review economy and neoliberal public relations.

Notes

1 Hiebert, J. (2016, April). "Consumer reports in the age of the Amazon review." *The Atlantic*. Retrieved from: www.theatlantic.com/business/archive/2016/04/consumer-reports-in-the-age-of-the-amazon-review/477108/.
2 Hiebert, J. (2016, April).
3 Pérez-Peña, P. (2007, December 8). "Success without ads." *The New York Times*. Retrieved from: www.nytimes.com/2007/12/08/business/media/08consumer.html.
4 *Consumer Reports*. (2017, January 12). "Consumer Reports now recommends MacBook Pros." *Consumer Reports*. Retrieved from: www.consumerreports.org/apple/consumer-reports-now-recommends-macbook-pros/.
5 *Consumer Reports*. (2019). "No commercial use policy." *Consumer Reports*. Retrieved from: www.consumerreports.org/cro/about-us/policies-and-financials/no-commercial-use-policy/index.htm.
6 Hiebert, J. (2016, April).
7 *Consumer Reports*. (2019).
8 *Chatmeter*. (2019). "The history of online business reviews." *Chatmeter*. Retrieved from: www.chatmeter.com/blog/the-history-of-online-business-reviews/.
9 Capoccia, C. (2018, April 11). "Online reviews are the best thing that ever happened to small businesses." *Forbes*. Retrieved from: www.forbes.com/sites/forbestechcouncil/2018/04/11/online-reviews-are-the-best-thing-that-ever-happened-to-small-businesses/#44f949c740a0.
10 Mudambi, S. M., Schuff, D., & Zhang, Z. (2014). "Why aren't the stars aligned? An analysis of online review content and star ratings." Paper presented at HICSS, 3139–3147. doi:10.1109/HICSS.2014.389.
11 Zhou, W., & Duan, W. (2015). "An empirical study of how third-party websites influence the feedback mechanism between online word-of-mouth and retail sales." *Decision Support Systems*, 76, 14. doi:10.1016/j.dss.2015.03.010.
12 Zhou, W., & Duan, W. (2015).
13 Zhou, W., & Duan, W. (2015).
14 Mudambi, S. M. et al. (2014).
15 Lee, H., & Blum, S. C. (2015). "How hotel responses to online reviews differ by hotel rating: An exploratory study." *Worldwide Hospitality and Tourism Themes*, 7(3), 242–250. doi:10.1108/WHATT-03-2015-0016.
16 Novak, A. N. (2016). "The revenge of Cecil the Lion: Credibility in online third-party review sites." In Folk, M., & Apostel, S. (Eds.) *Establishing and evaluating digital ethos and online credibility*. Hershey, PA: IGI Global.
17 Denizci Guillet, B., & Law, R. (2010). "Analyzing hotel star ratings on third-party distribution websites." *International Journal of Contemporary Hospitality Management*, 22(6), 797–813. doi:10.1108/09596111011063098.
18 Novak, A. N. (2016).
19 Novak, A. N. (2016).
20 Novak, A. N. (2016).

21 Shaffer, G., & Zettelmeyer, F. (2002). "When good news about your rival is good for you: The effect of third-party information on the division of channel profits." *Marketing Science*, 21(3), 273–293. doi:10.1287/mksc.21.3.273.137.

22 Sperber, J. (2014). "Yelp and labor discipline: How the internet works for capitalism." *New Labor Forum*, 23(2), 68–74. doi:10.1177/1095796014527066.

23 Sperber, J. (2014).

24 Kuehn, K. M. (2016). "Branding the self on yelp: Consumer reviewing as image entrepreneurship." *Social Media + Society*, 2(4). doi:10.1177/2056305116678895.

25 Kuehn, K. M. (2016).

26 Goldsmith, J., & Wu, T. (2008). *Who controls the internet? Illusions of a borderless world.* Oxford: Oxford University Press.

27 Kuehn, K. M. (2013). "'There's got to be a review democracy': Communicative capitalism, neoliberal citizenship and the politics of participation on the consumer evaluation website yelp.com." *International Journal of Communication* (Online), 607.

28 Kuehn, K. M. (2013).

29 Cockayne, D. G. (2016). "Sharing and neoliberal discourse: The economic function of sharing in the digital on-demand economy." *Geoforum*, 77, 73–82. doi:10.1016/j.geoforum.2016.10.005.

30 Cockayne, D. G. (2016).

31 Stemler, A. (2016). "Betwixt and between: Regulating the shared economy." *Fordham Urban Law Journal*, 43(1), 31.

32 Caldiero, C. (2015). *Neo-PR: Public relations in a postmodern world.* Peter Lang: New York.

33 Krinsky, J. (2011). "Neoliberal times: Intersecting temporalities and the neoliberalization of New York City's public-sector labor relations." *Social Science History*, 35(3), 381–422. doi:10.1215/01455532-1273348.

34 Ilcan, S. (2009). "Privatizing responsibility: Public sector reform under neoliberal government." *Canadian Review of Sociology*, 46(3), 207–234. doi:10.1111/j.1755-618X.2009.01212.x.

35 Caldiero, C. (2015).

36 Ilcan, S. (2009).

37 Kuehn, K. M. (2013).

38 Caldiero, C. (2015).

39 Miraftab, F. (2004). "Public–private partnerships: The Trojan horse of neoliberal development?" *Journal of Planning Education and Research*, 24(1), 89–101. doi:10.1177/0739456X04267173.

40 Caldiero, C. (2015).

41 Caldiero, C. (2015).

42 Caldiero, C. (2015); Savini, F. (2017). "Planning, uncertainty and risk: The neoliberal logics of Amsterdam urbanism." *Environment and Planning A*, 49(4), 857–875. doi:10.1177/0308518X16684520.

43 Savini, F. (2017).

44 Caldiero, C. (2015); Savini, F. (2017); Miraftab, F. (2004).
45 Winslow, L. (2016). "Doing more with less: Modeling neoliberal labor relations in Undercover Boss." *The Journal of Popular Culture*, 49(6), 1357–1374. doi:10.1111/jpcu.12496.
46 Winslow, L. (2016).
47 Winslow, L. (2016); Hardey, M. (2010). "Consuming professions: User-review websites and health services." *Journal of Consumer Culture*, 10(1), 129–149. doi:10.1177/1469540509355023.
48 Hardey, M. (2010); Hadiz, V. R. (2004). "Indonesian local party politics: A site of resistance to neoliberal reform." *Critical Asian Studies*, 36(4), 615–636. doi:10.1080/1467271042000273275; McCafferty, P. (2010). "Forging a 'neoliberal pedagogy': The 'enterprising education' agenda in schools." *Critical Social Policy*, 30(4), 541–563. doi:10.1177/0261018310376802.
49 Caldiero, C. (2015).
50 Richmond, M. A., & Garmany, J. (2016). "'Post-third-world city' or neoliberal 'city of exception'? Rio de Janeiro in the Olympic era." *International Journal of Urban and Regional Research*, 40(3), 621–639. doi:10.1111/1468-2427.12338.
51 Richmond, M. A., & Garmany, J. (2016).
52 Miraftab, F. (2004).
53 Miraftab, F. (2004); Richmond, M. A., & Garmany, J. (2016).
54 Richmond, M. A., & Garmany, J. (2016).
55 *Podium*. (2019). "5 advantages to Google reviews." *Podium*. Retrieved from: www.podium.com/google-reviews/5-advantages-google-reviews/.
56 *Podium*. (2019).
57 Khan, H. (2018, February 7). "How online reviews impact local SEO and why they matter to your bottom line." *Shopify*. Retrieved from: www.shopify.com/retail/119916611-how-online-reviews-impact-local-seo-and-why-they-matter-to-your-bottom-line.
58 Tsukayama, H. (2013, May 22). "How much power does a Yelp review have?" *The Washington Post*. Retrieved from: www.washingtonpost.com/business/technology/how-much-power-does-a-yelp-review-have/2013/05/22/6b8f961c-c210-11e2-8c3b-0b5e9247e8ca_story.html.
59 Bowman, M. (2019, January 15). "Online reviews and their impact on the bottom line." *Forbes*. Retrieved from: www.forbes.com/sites/forbesagencycouncil/2019/01/15/online-reviews-and-their-impact-on-the-bottom-line/#67caf1e95bde.
60 Hinckley, D. (2015, September 5). "New study: Data reveals 67% of consumers are influenced by online reviews." *Moz*. Retrieved from: https://moz.com/blog/new-data-reveals-67-of-consumers-are-influenced-by-online-reviews.
61 Sussman, S., Garcia, R., Cruz, T. B. et al. (2014). "Consumers' perceptions of vape shops in Southern California: An analysis of online Yelp reviews." *Tobacco Induced Diseases*, 12(1), 22. doi:10.1186/s12971-014-0022-7.

1 Digital Labor on Third-Party Review Sites

In early 1999, a software developer looking for a hobby launched "TeacherRatings.com," a digital platform that allowed students to rate faculty members in North America and the UK. By 2001, the site was re-branded to its now infamous name, "Rate My Professors," known worldwide by faculty and students looking for information before registering for classes.[1] Students can leave or read reviews on existing faculty pages with details about professor availability, course difficulty, and textbook use. The TPRS also premiered the "tamale," a red pepper that appeared on professor pages if students found them attractive.[2] Today, the platform also features annual rankings of schools based on student reviews including "best campus eats" and "colorful professionals" which features faculty with colorful names.

The site is both beloved and feared by faculty, students, and administrators. In a 2018 article from *University Wire*, professors sounded off about frustrations from the site.[3] Many reflected that most evaluation platforms tend to reflect how students feel about the professor's personality not the quality or quantity of work included in the class. Others voiced concerns that the platform encouraged harassment and abuse from vengeful students, "'How would students feel if we put up a website that was ratemystudent.com?' Professor of English Lisa Sánchez asked. 'It seems to me like a recipe … at least from the faculty point of view, for harassment and nastiness.'"[4] Other faculty reflected that validity of reviews (whether collected formally, in class, or through an external digital platform) is flawed and well documented by academic research.[5] However, the same article found that students widely disagreed with these professor concerns, often reflecting that the site was helpful as they selected classes, bought textbooks, or studied for midterms. As hundreds of other editorials and blogs featured about Rate My Professors demonstrate, there are widely varying viewpoints on the usefulness and credibility of the site. Despite these mixed reviews, today,

Rate My Professors is the largest warehouse of teacher ratings around the world, with over 19 million ratings, 7,500 schools, and 1.7 million teachers rated on its site.[6] In many ways, the controversies over Rate My Professors reflect larger tensions that exist within TPRS and digital labor. First, debates over the reliability and helpfulness of TPRS exist in almost every industry, often showcasing differences between the views of consumers and organizations. Second, TPRS require labor from consumers (or in Rate My Professors' case, students) to build content and provide robust information that meets user needs. Third, other users must validate and trust the labor from reviewers for TPRS to operate successfully. This labor is a key part of neoliberal public relations, or the use of the labor of consumers to drive both content of TPRS and organizational engagement.

Alongside the popularization of social media, TPRS such as Yelp, Google Reviews, and Rate My Professors proliferated as a digitized neoliberal force in promotional culture, public relations, and advertising. These sites encourage users to contribute to "the greater good" and labor to provide information that may help other members of the public make informed decisions. TPRS use a neoliberal design that suggests users may (or may not) get immediate gratification for labor and publishing a review of a business, but by helping other members of the public, they contribute to the overall success or failure of a deserving company – thus benefiting their own vision of the world.

The neoliberal labor exhibited on TPRS was a key part of the emergence and growth of similar platforms since the early 1990s. Like Rate My Professors, early TPRS required consumers to provide reviews for the consumption of other users and readers. Over the first decade of popularity, TPRS became havens of neoliberal labor and the potential of digital engagement. This chapter describes both the history of labor on TPRS and how today's TPRS are structurally designed to maximize the potential of user contributions and engagement.

Emergence and Growth of TPRS

Two of the earliest TPRS were Epinion and Deja.com.[7] Created during the 1990s' dotcom boom, the sites were some of the earliest spaces where users could turn for information about specific products or services before a purchase.[8] Deja.com was started in 1995 as an extension of the popular *Usenet* website, an online system where users could post and read messages (similar to bulletin board systems) or what eventually became Internet forums (still used today).[9] Deja.com provided users a way to search Usenet, a critical function since Usenet had no central server or formal moderator.[10] These archives could be searched for posts about a specific product or service and were particularly popular for discussions of software glitches and updates. By 1999, Deja. com transitioned to a shopping-comparison site dedicated to helping users make informed purchase decisions. Its "before you buy" motto was prominently displayed on store windows and even on product packaging by organizations that wanted to boast about positive reviews or information.[11]

However, due to financial crises, Deja.com was dismantled and shut down in 2001. eBay and half.com acquired its shopping comparison site, and Google purchased the Usenet archive and search infrastructure.[12] By 2005, Deja.com and Usenet transformed into Google Groups – promoted by any search engine's suggestion to access Google Groups instead of either platform after a web search.

One of the other popular TPRS during the 1990s, Epinions, was established as a way for users to search reviews of products and organizations before making a purchase. The platform was created by several prominent figures from the dotcom bubble including Yahoo, Netscape, and McKinsey executives.[13] Despite over 5.8 million users, Epinions struggled to make a profit and by 2003 it was acquired by Dealtime, then Shopping.com, and then eBay in 2005. Although it was operational until 2014, eBay announced it would dismantle Epinions, including all usernames and accounts.[14] Today, searching for the site redirects you to Shopping.com or eBay.

Epinions and Deja.com are similar in that both sites grew rapidly in popularity because of the public perception that giving reviews would help others make purchase decisions. With millions of users (even during the beginnings of Internet popularity), each site boasted millions of reviews and messages for readers to utilize when planning. However, both struggled with a key aspect of running an online platform: making money. As Nirav Tolia, one of the founders of Epinions reflected, "We felt we couldn't finish what we started because we had a little problem. We needed a viable business model."[15] Despite their popularity, early TPRS did not know how to monetize user labor or engagement in an effective way. As a result, the platforms were bought out by much larger corporations that could embed TPRS features within existing infrastructures.

This buyout was another key similarity between the earliest TPRS. Although both Epinions and Deja.com were initially started by dotcom professionals, their success (at getting user engagement and attention) made them attractive to much larger digital conglomerates such as Google, Yahoo, and eBay. Without "viable business models," early TPRS were frequently bought by these larger companies, which sought to integrate features of the sites into already-profitable parts of their business. As a result, there are relatively few independent TPRS platforms today. Nearly all are owned by other digital conglomerates – albeit often hidden ownership structures from the public. This reduces the number of TPRS competitors and allows large conglomerates to monetize digital labor effectively.

Although Google purchased dozens of smaller TPRS like Deja.com, it failed to acquire the fastest growing TPRS in the early 2000s, Yelp. Within its first five years of operations (2004–2009), Yelp transformed the prominence and profitability of TPRS. Despite initial talks of acquisition in 2009, Yelp avoided being bought out by Google, and instead became a publicly traded company.[16] But how did it become profitable? It started selling advertising space on its site, allowing companies to pay to promote their companies as first on search lists within a specific market. This simple transformation allowed the company to become both profitable and controversial as it sacrificed public control over organizational messaging in exchange for money.[17] Despite some early journalistic criticism and concerns over public acceptance of advertising content on the site, Yelp's popularity continued to grow and today it boasts nearly 192 million reviews. As a result, Google and Yelp are two of the largest TPRS in the world, competing for advertising revenue, public engagement, and labor.

Despite their dominance, smaller TPRS also boast popularity within more specific markets and industries. Like Rate My Professors' use by students and faculty, other industries have their own sites and platforms. For example, Angie's List offers reviews for home repair/service contractors; TripAdvisor offers reviews on travel companies, hotels, and tourist attractions; and, Glassdoor allows employees to review employers and share information with prospective applicants. Like the histories of deja.com and Epinions with Google and Yelp, these industry-specific TPRS are owned by larger conglomerates, but operate as independent websites. Additionally, they all require neoliberal labor to operate.

Neoliberal Public Relations, Labor, and Public Engagement

Neoliberal labor is the effort of users contributing capital into a digital space to benefit other users or consumers.[18] When users provide reviews to TPRS, they contribute their capital or resources in the form of time, knowledge, and opinions.[19] The effort involved in translating these opinions and knowledge into review posts is known as labor.[20]

Users who provide reviews are called "contributors" because of the labor they give to the site. Unlike most forms of physical labor, the digital labor performed by contributors is unpaid in a monetary way, so instead contributors must hold other motivations for their work. Novak reflects that there are three major motivations for submitting reviews to TPRS.[21] First, contributors want to share their experiences to help others make informed decisions. Second, contributors want to correct misinformation from advertising or other public relations initiatives. And third, contributors want to elicit change within an organization, thus giving future customers a better experience. These three reasons describe the neoliberal intentions of TPRS contributors. These neoliberal intentions illustrate that most reviewers see others as directly benefiting from their contributions, while they themselves indirectly benefit by the culture of reviewing. Reviews are directly intended to help readers make purchasing decisions. However, by participating in TPRS, contributors have an indirect expectation that they will also benefit from the labor of other contributors. While their labor does not directly benefit their own purchasing decisions, they accept the labor of other contributors as enhancing their own decision-making.

At the heart of neoliberalism is the exchange of labor (often in a digital form) for minor forms of cultural change that indirectly benefit the contributor.[22] The goal for many contributors is to work alongside an infinite number of other contributors to collaborate and impact organizational practices and relationships. Neoliberal labor is the vehicle for this change and requires buy-in from other contributors as well as readers and organizations.[23] There must be a system to hold reviews, a culture of acceptance of reviews by organization, and an appreciation of reviews by users. This neoliberal labor is the foundation of today's review economy and is prominent in many TPRS.

In addition to contributors, other users are also critical to the impact of neoliberal labor. Readers must value these reviews by visiting the sites, looking up organizations before making purchasing decisions, upvoting or commenting on helpful or unhelpful reviews, and eventually becoming contributors themselves by sharing information from their own experiences. In short, readers also perform labor on the site by dedicating their capital (time and attention).

But how do TPRS cultivate digital labor into daily practices on their sites? For TPRS, building a platform that encourages contributors to perform digital labor, and readers to engage the platform for information-gathering practices, is critical. Through a grounded theory approach, this chapter looks at how Yelp reinforces digital labor practices.

Platform Design and Neoliberal Labor

To study how Yelp uses intersectionality in its platform design to encourage a relationship between organizations and reviewers, this chapter uses a grounded theory approach. Gasson and Waters position grounded theory as an ideal way to study online spaces and identity.[24] Grounded theory in digital spaces argues that researchers inductively study an online platform to produce conceptual categories related to identity formation, promotional practices, and online discourse.[25] The methodology is particularly helpful in studies of digital spaces where users co-construct messaging and discourses, such as message boards, social media, and wikis.[26] In this chapter, Yelp is investigated using a grounded theory approach because of previous scholarship on TPRS that support its rigor and insight.[27,28,29]

Yelp was selected as the foci of this study due to its prominence in the reviewer economy and popularity.[30,31] Yelp is the largest online TPRS, boasting nearly 192 million global reviews, and over 100 million unique visitors a month. Zhu et al. note that Yelp's power in the industry comes not just from its popularity, but also the amount of trust users place in the accuracy and honesty of site recommendations.[32] In a study comparing online review effectiveness, the depth and length of Yelp reviews deemed them more trustworthy than the average reviews on Google Reviews and Facebook.[33] Further, scholars measuring the effectiveness of Yelp note that just a one-star deduction in average rating can produce a 10 percent loss in profit, thus demonstrating the site's impact on organizational practices and effectiveness.[34] Its popularity with information-seeking public and potential impact on organizational success make Yelp an ideal site to study intersectionality.

Yelp's Positioning

Immediately evident from Yelp's site is how the TPRS positions itself as a digital space for communities to build relationships and express opinions across demographic and geographic boundaries. The diversity of users is referred to eight times in Yelp's "about us" section of the website as "unique," demonstrating the desire to identify users not based on demographic attributes or categories, but instead as beyond identifier or common background. Previous research on neoliberal design notes that organizations who move beyond traditional demographic categorization adopt an intersectional design where identity is less about physicality and more about subject-positioning and community development.[35] This is further established by the relatively little identifying information needed when setting up a new Yelp account. New users only need to provide their name, zip code, and email address (adding a birth date is optional). Again, previous scholarship notes that reduced demographic information at the point of entry to a new site is indicative of an intersectional design that does not require categorization of identifiers such as gender, age, or race/ethnicity.[36] While other Yelp scholars note that the platform does not need to ask for this information since they are likely to triangulate it by examining user data (such as the businesses visited), the combination of referring to users as unique and beyond categorization reflects an intersectional design.[37]

Beyond reflections on self and identity within Yelp's design, the site positions itself as a bridge between local businesses and users. In a sentence, Yelp's mission is to "To connect people with great local businesses."[38] Yelp articulates its goal to bring local businesses closer to individuals as they seek information before making purchase decisions. Yelp expands upon this mission in its FAQ page by explaining it was started to help customers find new businesses that could otherwise be drowned out by large, well-known companies. As a platform, the site intended to give users a place to make recommendations for those small unknown businesses to make it easier for other interested future customers to find it. This mission reflects the neoliberal drive to return commercial power to customers and affirm the review economy.[39]

In addition to expressing this neoliberal philosophy throughout its "about us" and FAQ pages, Yelp incorporates this position into the design of its review pages. Yelp uses a "recommended reviews" page based on community feedback to identify and promote recommended reviews for each business profile. Initially, recommended reviews were selected by a computer algorithm; however, today's Yelp platform uses upvoting to measure the popularity and usefulness of each review. Reviews that are "upvoted" by readers are then pushed higher into the archived list of reviews. The reviews with the most upvotes appear first in the profile and receive a star badge that designates them as "selected by the community." Yelp explains this process and rationale in its "recommended reviews" FAQ page. Yelp positions this feature to give users more control over the reviewing process and the information given out first by an organization. Scholars note that in TPRS, readers rarely read beyond the first eight reviews, thus upvoted reviews get more attention and are selected to represent the larger reviewing community.[40] Yelp implies that upvoting gives control over the first reviews in any profile to users, rather than the businesses or companies being reviewed. As noted by Stemler, Yelp positions itself as returning reputational control and information control to users, thus taking it away from traditional commercial approaches.[41]

Previous scholarship on Yelp identifies a history of scrubbing, where an organization can pay the site to remove or bury negative reviews so they are difficult to find by users.[42] Throughout Yelp's background pages, there are repeated references to Yelp's new policies against scrubbing and its dedication to providing accurate feedback, regardless of Yelp's relationship with businesses. Yelp reflects in its section on "recommended reviews" that "In short, there is no relationship between reviews and anything having to do with Yelp Ads or the Yelp Ads sales process." In addition, the site provides an infographic that depicts how ad sales work and how they are not related to review appearance or quality of information (Advertiser FAQ). Although there are no references to prior scrubbing-based lawsuits, the site is quick to position itself as honest and independent. To support this argument, it cites and links to independent academic research:

> An independent academic study (not commissioned or paid for by Yelp) found that advertising plays no role in how reviews are recommended on Yelp. Or as this in-depth profile of Yelp in *BuzzFeed* puts it: "Harvard Business School professor Michael Luca has co-authored a new study that effectively debunks the extortion theory."

Yelp uses extensive supporting evidence explaining the relationship of advertising sales to bolster its site credibility, particularly as rumors and a history of scrubbing challenge its reputation and user trust.[43] While the frequent reflections that the site no longer uses either practice could be interpreted as "over-compensation," at the very least, the site positions itself as an honest reflection of public opinion, thus returning the power of the reviewer economy to users.

Scrubbing is a direct challenge to the neoliberal design of Yelp, thus giving the site a good reason to want to position itself as honest and accurate. While the neoliberal design gives the power of reputation to consumers, scrubbing returns it to the businesses but gives the illusion of control to users. Previous scholarship deems scrubbing unethical and diminishes the trust between the TPRS and users.[44] Thus, Yelp addresses scrubbing throughout its background pages to prevent users from questioning this digital practice. This upfront response to scrubbing allegations positions the organizations as aligning with neoliberal demands for user control and transparency. While Yelp articulates these positions within its "about us" sections, this is also viewed in the platform design and affordances – examined in the next section.

Yelp's Affordances

Affordances are design features of a web platform that encourage specific user behaviors and discourage other practices.[45] For example, users are encouraged to like or approve of posts on Facebook through a "thumbs-up" button at the bottom of each post.[46] Similarly, TPRS use affordances to encourage user behavior through the structural design of the platform (i.e. buttons, links, upvoting).[47]

As noted in previous studies, Yelp's platform encourages user engagement throughout each business profile. The first structural options of the page include links to "write a review," "add a picture," "share," the page, and "bookmark" for future use. These options provide opportunities for users to engage the profile, even if they are not leaving their own review. They demonstrate the neoliberal design of the space by providing users options to seek and share information with a larger community – even on other social media platforms (the share button allows users to share a profile on Twitter, Facebook, and via email).

The second section of a business profile also adopts a neoliberal design as it allows users and business owners to co-construct information about the business. While business owners can "claim a page" and then update store hours, official pictures, and menus (if applicable), users are encouraged to edit or suggest revisions to this information if they see there are inaccuracies. For example, one user posted a comment stating that a local café's hours were different during the summer weekends than the information posted on Yelp. Aaron Richmond and Garmany argue that this co-construction of information is vital to the neoliberal economy because it gives both parties control over publicity and accuracy.[48] Yelp's affordances make co-construction (where both parties are encouraged to update a profile and share the reputation responsibilities), a priority on the website. New users are encouraged in the "welcome email" to contribute reviews and update business information as they see fit, thus helping to improve the accuracy and helpfulness of the TPRS.

In the third section of a business profile, an "ask the community" section allows users to post questions of a business. Examples include, "what should I get to eat?" and "Who is the best barber on Wednesdays?" Questions like these can be answered by either the business owner or reviewers, again, a co-construction affordance of the site.

The final section of a business profile is controlled only by users; modification is not allowed by business owners or affiliates (as instructed in the rules and regulations pages). Here, the bulk of the reviewing process takes place including asking recent customers for reviews, upvoting for helpful reviews, and archiving older or non-recommended reviews. Readers can demonstrate their approval or appreciation of a review by clicking "useful," "funny," or "cool" (or some combination). The reviews with the most votes (from combining the categories) appear at the top of the list of reviews in decreasing popularity. These buttons encourage the neoliberal design and function of Yelp as they provide feedback not only to the businesses (through the reviews themselves), but also to the reviewers so that they can improve their reflections in the future.[49] Zhou and Duan note that this ongoing feedback to make the platform more helpful and accurate is part of the neoliberal intention of the space.[50] The feedback given to both business owners and the reviewers encourages users to trust the space for information on future purchase decisions.

Importantly, reviews are not restricted by size, and (generally) longer reviews receive more upvotes than shorter ones, thus encouraging users to provide deeper insight and lengthy reflection in their posts. This practice is also encouraged by Yelp's elite program (discussed in the next section) that rewards reviewers for the depth of the reviews and time dedicated to reviewing.

Finally, social networking affordances are also incorporated into the design of each review and user profile, thus encouraging users to communicate and engage each other. Users can "follow" each other, meaning they see each other's reviews upon logging in on the home screen. In addition, users can message each other privately or send each other "compliments." These affordances encourage positive interaction behaviors between users oriented around the quality of reviews and review helpfulness. Networking is critical in intersectional design because it encourages users to form communities not based on physical attributes; rather, partnerships form around shared interests. This transcendence of demographic categories, as replaced by a desire to improve the information on Yelp, is afforded by the networking capabilities and affordances of Yelp.[51] In the following section, networking is explored as a practice, with attention to how this practice is encouraged.

Yelp's Practices

While all users (unless banned from the site) are encouraged to provide reviews and engage business profiles, Yelp developed programs to reward especially dedicated reviewers and contributors. The Yelp Elite Squad (YES) is a selection of top reviewers from each city or region, who receive perks for their participation in the TPRS. YES members are selected by Yelp management based on the number of reviews they generate, how long they were members of the site, how many followers they have, how many compliments they receive, and their thoroughness in each review. Users can apply to become YES members, but they must be approved by site management. YES members have a small "Elite" badge, along with the year they were awarded elite status, which appears on their profile and under each review. YES members are frequently invited on "elite-only" experiences, including special happy hours, promotional events, and business grand openings. Because they are recognized for the high quality of their reviews, businesses covet their attention and engagement when looking to improve their reputation on the site.

The YES program at first seems counter-intuitive to an intersectional design because of its promotion and recognition of some reviewers as more important than others. However, the intention of the YES program is to encourage more intersectional and neoliberal practices on the site by providing users with a goal. Beyond the communal goal of making Yelp more helpful and accurate to information seekers, it provides an individual goal of improved status and social capital associated with YES membership. In short, it gives additional incentives for users to contribute to the site and engage other users positively.

YES membership also encourages intersectional identity because of its commitment to recognizing "unique voices" on the platform. The YES FAQ page reflects that the program values diversity in experience and voice, and selects members based on the breadth and depth of customer experiences and businesses reviewed. Early criticism of YES argued that it valued individuals from higher socio-economic backgrounds and more free time because it rewards those who can perform free labor and those who have the resources to engage a variety of experiences (some costing a great deal).[52] While Yelp does not directly respond to this criticism, its continued reference to diversity in voice in the YES program transcends the traditional demographic categories and reflects on a more intersectional observation of identity. Although Yelp users can provide additional demographic information when applying for YES, Yelp notes they are more interested in the personal essay that reflects on why TPRS matter to the user and their community.

Yelp also maintains other practices that encourage the neoliberal intentions of the site and information sharing. For example, the site can ban users who violate the extensive end-user license agreements on the site. Behaviors that result in banning include: lying in reviews, posting lewd or inappropriate content, trolling other users, posting fake reviews for money, and sabotaging competitors' reviews. Importantly, there is little that Yelp can do to ensure these banned users do not create new accounts because of the limited identifying information collected when setting up a new account. Here the intersectional design of the platform may hinder its later practice of banning users performing outside of the norms and rules of the site.

Because of Yelp's prominence and popularity as a source of information for consumers, it is one of the most important parts of the review economy. However, other platforms with more industry-specific foci, such as Angie's List, are also critical to understanding how concepts like credibility and trust impact the review economy. This is the focus of the next chapter.

Notes

1 Ritter, K. (2008). "E-valuating learning: Rate My Professors and public rhetorics of pedagogy." *Rhetoric Review*, 27(3), 259–280. Retrieved from: https://doi.org/10.1080/07350190802126177.
2 Simpson, D., Henningsen, M., Bryan, F., & Valde, K. (2019). "Rate My Professors: Electronic word of mouth and expectancy violations theory in the classroom." (ProQuest Dissertations Publishing). Retrieved from: http://search.proquest.com/docview/2247976136/.
3 Santillo, S. (2018, November 16). "How does Rate My Professors rate with students and professors? Views from both sides of the Lecture Hall." *University Wire*. Retrieved from: https://search.proquest.com/docview/2134086753.
4 Santillo, S. (2018, November 16).
5 Santillo, S. (2018, November 16).
6 RateMyProfessors (2020). "About us." *Ratemyprofessors.com.* Retrieved from: www.ratemyprofessors.com/About.jsp.
7 Barrett, A. (1999). "What's your epinion? On epinions.com, read product reviews by regular folks, then post your own." (Company Business and Marketing). Network World.
8 Riedman, P. (1999). "Deja.com hypes reviews with $10 mil campaign." *Advertising Age*, 70(20), 52. Retrieved from: http://search.proquest.com/docview/208370224/.
9 Riedman, P. (1999).
10 Weil, N. (2001). "Google buys Usenet from Deja.com." (Company Business and Marketing). Network World.
11 Weil, N. (2001).

12 Bronstad, A. (2000). "Downsized Deja.com nears finalizing of sale." *Austin Business Journal*, 20(35), 8. Retrieved from: http://search.proquest.com/docview/218352495/.

13 Bronson, P. (1999, July 11). "Instant company." *The New York Times Magazine*. Retrieved from: www.nytimes.com/1999/07/11/magazine/instant-company.html?pagewanted=all&ref=magazine.

14 Mackiewicz, J. (2011). "Epinions advisors as technical editors: Using politeness across levels of edit." *Journal of Business and Technical Communication*, 25(4), 421–448. Retrieved from: https://doi.org/10.1177/1050651911411038.

15 Hansell, S. (2003, March 12). "Dealtime agrees to buy Epinions." *The New York Times*. Retrieved from: www.newyorktimes.com/ffik2818.

16 Heine, C. (2013). "Yelp CEO doesn't fear Foursquare." *Adweek*, 54(29), 15. Retrieved from: http://search.proquest.com/docview/1432023292/.

17 Pentina, I., Bailey, A., & Zhang, L. (2018). "Exploring effects of source similarity, message valence, and receiver regulatory focus on Yelp review persuasiveness and purchase intentions." *Journal of Marketing Communications*, 24(2), 125–145. Retrieved from: https://doi.org/10.1080/13527266.2015.1005115.

18 Dumitrica, D., & Wyatt, S. (2015). "Digital technologies and social transformations: What role for critical theory?" *Canadian Journal of Communication*, 40(4), 589–596. Retrieved from: https://doi.org/10.22230/cjc.2015v40n4a3044.

19 van Doorn, N. (2014). "The neoliberal subject of value: Measuring human capital in information economies." *Cultural Politics: An International Journal*, 10(3), 354–375. Retrieved from: https://doi.org/10.1215/17432197-2795729.

20 Vanderhoef, J. (2016). "An industry of Indies: The new cultural economy of digital game production." Dissertation. Retrieved from: www.escholarship.org/uc/item/9vc0q914.

21 Novak, A. N. (2016). "The revenge of Cecil the Lion: Credibility in online third-party review sites." In Folk, M., & Apostel, S. (Eds.) *Establishing and evaluating digital ethos and online credibility*. Hershey, PA: IGI Global.

22 Rossi, U. (2019). "The common-seekers: Capturing and reclaiming value in the platform metropolis." *Environment and Planning C: Politics and Space*, 37(8), 1418–1433. Retrieved from: https://doi.org/10.1177/2399654419830975.

23 Hardey, M. (2010). "Consuming professions: User-review websites and health services." *Journal of Consumer Culture*, 10(1), 129–149. Retrieved from: https://doi.org/10.1177/1469540509355023.

24 Gasson, S., & Waters, J. (2013). "Using a grounded theory approach to study online collaboration behaviors." *European Journal of Information Systems*, 22(1), 95–118. Retrieved from: https://doi.org/10.1057/ejis.2011.24.

25 Pentzold, C. (2011). "Imagining the Wikipedia community: What do Wikipedia authors mean when they write about their 'community'?" *New Media & Society*, 13(5), 704–721. doi:10.1177/1461444810378364.

26 Pentzold, C. (2011).

27 Kuehn, K. M. (2016). "Branding the self on Yelp: Consumer reviewing as image entrepreneurship." *Social Media + Society*, 2(4). doi:10.1177/2056305116678895.

28 Kilaru, A. S., Meisel, Z. F., Paciotti, B., Ha, Y. P., Smith, R. J., Ranard, B. L., & Merchant, R. M. (2016). "What do patients say about emergency departments in online reviews? A qualitative study." *British Medical Journal Quality & Safety*, 25(1), 14–24. doi:10.1136/bmjqs-2015–004035.

29 Krasnova, H., Veltri, N. F., Spengler, K., & Günther, O. (2013). "'Deal of the day' platforms: What drives consumer loyalty?" *Business & Information Systems Engineering*, 5(3), 165–177. doi:10.1007/s12599-013-0268-2.

30 Sperber, J. (2014). "Yelp and labor discipline: How the internet works for capitalism." *New Labor Forum*, 23(2), 68–74. doi:10.1177/1095796014527066.

31 Kuehn, K. M. (2016).

32 Zhu, L., Yin, G., & He, W. (2014). "Is this opinion leader's review useful? Peripheral cues for online review helpfulness." *Journal of Electronic Commerce Research*, 15(4), 267–280.

33 Zhu, L. et al. (2014).

34 Cockayne, D. G. (2016). "Sharing and neoliberal discourse: The economic function of sharing in the digital on-demand economy." *Geoforum*, 77, 73–82. doi:10.1016/j.geoforum.2016.10.005.

35 Dy, A. M., Marlow, S., & Martin, L. (2017). "A web of opportunity or the same old story? Women digital entrepreneurs and intersectionality theory." *Human Relations*, 70(3), 286–311. doi:10.1177/0018726716650730.

   Leurs, K., Midden, E., & Ponzanesi, S. (2011). "Digital multiculturalism in the Netherlands: Religious, ethnic, and gender positioning by Moroccan–Dutch youth." *Religion and Gender*, 2(1), 150–175. doi:10.18352/rg.36.

36 Leurs, K. et al. (2011).

37 Kuehn, K. M. (2016).

38 Yelp. (2020). "About us" *Yelp.com*. Retrieved from: www.Yelp.com/aboutus.

39 Cockayne, D. G. (2016).

40 Ziniel, W. (2014). *Third party product reviews and consumer behavior: A dichotomous measuring via rasch, paired comparison and graphical chain models* (1st ed.). Wiesbaden: Springer Gabler.

41 Stemler, A. (2016). "Betwixt and between: Regulating the shared economy." *Fordham Urban Law Journal*, 43(1), 31.

42 Novak, A. N. (2016). "The revenge of Cecil the Lion: Credibility in online third-party review sites." In Folk, M., & Apostel, S. (Eds.) *Establishing and evaluating digital ethos and online credibility.* Hershey, PA: IGI Global.

43 Novak, A. N. (2016).

44 Novak, A. N. (2016).

45 Majchrzak, A., Faraj, S., Kane, G. C., & Azad, B. (2013). "The contradictory influence of social media affordances on online communal knowledge sharing." *Journal of Computer-Mediated Communication*, 19(1), 38–55. doi:10.1111/jcc4.12030.

46 Vaast, E., & Kaganer, E. (2013). "Social media affordances and governance in the workplace: An examination of organizational policies." *Journal of Computer-Mediated Communication*, 19(1), 78–101. doi:10.1111/jcc4.12032.
47 Majchrzak, A. et al. (2013); Zhou, W., & Duan, W. (2015). "An empirical study of how third-party websites influence the feedback mechanism between online word-of-mouth and retail sales." *Decision Support Systems*, 76, 14. doi:10.1016/j.dss.2015.03.010.
48 Richmond, M. A., & Garmany, J. (2016). "'Post-third-world city' or neoliberal 'city of exception'? Rio de Janeiro in the Olympic era." *International Journal of Urban and Regional Research*, 40(3), 621–639. doi:10.1111/1468-2427.12338.
49 Mudambi, S. M., Schuff, D., & Zhang, Z. (2014). "Why aren't the stars aligned? An analysis of online review content and star ratings." Paper presented at the 3139–3147. doi:10.1109/HICSS.2014.389.
50 Zhou, W., & Duan, W. (2015).
51 Okolosie, L. (2014). "Beyond 'talking' and 'owning' intersectionality." *Feminist Review*, 108(1), 90–96. doi:10.1057/fr.2014.14.
52 Askay, D. A., & Gossett, L. (2015). "Concealing communities within the crowd: Hiding organizational identities and brokering member identifications of the Yelp Elite Squad." *Management Communication Quarterly*, 29(4), 616–641. doi:10.1177/0893318915597301.

2 Trust, Credibility, and the Power of Reviews

In a March 2020 news release, Yelp announced it shut down 600 user accounts after identifying them as "fake" or "pay for review" accounts.[1] In an effort to combat a "growing problem" of fake reviews or artificially increased review scores, the platform is cracking down on accounts that it perceives as fake or operating against the pillars of honesty and transparency dictated by its end-user license agreement.

This massive deletion of fake accounts is part of a growing set of concerns that TPRS are increasingly manipulated by organizational action and intervention, rather than honest feedback from users. In short, the trust placed in TPRS by contributors, readers, and organizations is eroding, jeopardizing the perceived usefulness of reviews. Because TPRS are established as a constant source of information for consumers over the past two decades, the erosion of trust in these sites may greatly impact the review economy.

For the site, the erosion of trust may impact the number of users who regularly visit it. This would reduce the price of advertising (less visitors mean TPRS must charge less for advertising space), thus reducing the profitability of the platforms. For publicly traded companies like Yelp and Google, profitability is critical to the success of the organization and its longevity.

For readers, declining trust in TPRS means that the reviews are less valuable when making a purchase decision. If reviews are not considered trustworthy, then there is less incentive for the reader to turn to these sites when looking for products or services. It is possible that a new form of reviewing or review platform could take advantage of the declining trust in Google Reviews and Yelp and become a new source of information for readers.

Finally, for contributors a declining sense of trust in TPRS could impact their satisfaction in reviewing. If contributors feel like their reviews are not trusted, or that they must compete with fake reviews, they may be less likely to contribute. This erosion of trust could also diminish the neoliberal assumptions of reviewing, such as making the world better by informing others, or believing that a review culture indirectly also benefits reviewers.

Perhaps because of the increasing complications pertaining to trust on Yelp and Google Reviews, industry-specific TPRS have become popular sources of information. One of the largest, Angie's List, started in 1995 as a place for contributors to leave reviews for handymen and contractors. It started as a subscription-only service, requiring members to pay a monthly fee for access to both post and read reviews. As a part of the site, contractors who paid to be listed on the platform became "Angie's List Certified," a moniker they could list on personal websites, business cards, and other marketing content.

Although the platform opened its site to all in 2016, the initial paid-subscription style increased its appearance as a trustworthy and credible space for reviews. The platform also operated as an intermediary between critical contributors and organizations – often encouraging both parties to discuss problems, rectify them, and then remove the negative review.[2] The trust between the site and users is so critical to the success of Angie's List, it's the reason the company's slogan is: "Reviews You Can Trust."[3]

However, in order to understand the erosion of trust on some TPRS, and the cultivation of it on others, it is important to look at the type of people who contribute to the sites in the first place. This chapter examines how trust is developed between users and the platforms, and how this trust may be threatened by organizational practices or other forces.

Who Contributes to Reviews?

While TPRS' contributors are diverse and represent nearly every demographic category, scholars note that the motivations of users generate from a rather uniform intention.[4] Generally, TPRS posters reflect that they desired a space to provide feedback and participate in the public opinion formation process.[5] Gupta notes that TPRS are especially attractive to individuals who were previously or historically excluded from public opinion formation or were disadvantaged in more traditional public relations efforts.[6] Novak notes that one group, minority Millennials (born between 1981 and 2001), who ushered in the popularity of TPRS with their adoption of digital and social media, were especially attracted to TPRS reviews because it provided a space for them to impactfully contribute to the public opinion formation process.[7]

Minority Millennials were previously frustrated with the traditional campaigns of the 1980s and 1990s and biased attempts to paint the group as homogeneous, apathetic, and singularly focused on digital media.[8] Like social media, TPRS provided a space for minority Millennials to insert perspectives into the public opinion formation process without relying on traditional media campaigns.[9] Similarly, Tyler argues that feminist women adopted TPRS to influence public opinion away from traditional campaigns that they felt misrepresented their identity.[10] In fact, scholarship from around the world demonstrates that TPRS grew popular because segmented groups sought a way to influence public opinion outside of traditional media and campaigns.[11] These groups, who felt marginalized or excluded by traditional marketing and public relations efforts, used TPRS to insert their voice into a crowded media environment.[12]

Despite the research concluding that TPRS attract users who see themselves as part of marginalized groups, few studies considered specific demographic indicators of Yelp users. Tyler notes this may be a result of the intersection of identity in online spaces and the difficulty of researchers to use traditional demographic indicators in studying TPRS.[13] Dy et al. argue that online spaces construct identity as an intersection of many social categories, rather than a set of exclusive and exhaustive labels.[14] For marginalized groups, this intersectionality is appealing because of the history of exclusion and misidentification-based demographic categories.[15] McCormack and Anderson argue that online spaces shield users' visual demographic cues, thus giving users textual control over their digital appearance.[16] In a physical space, these visual cues encourage the audience to categorize a person with specific demographic labels, while in a digital space, the textual control given to the person allows them to use intersectional language and represent their identity as complexly as they desire.[17] Trahan demonstrates that while this intersectional identity can be liberating for individuals who felt previously marginalized by the categorization process, for researchers and practitioners, this can make studying identity in online spaces like TPRS especially challenging.[18] Else-Quest and Hyde argue that online intersectionality challenges traditional communication practices that focus on categorizing the public into exclusive and exhaustive segmented categories.[19] Thus, practitioners must learn how to develop communication strategies that recognize digital identity as a more complex intersectional entity than traditional promotional strategies posit.[20]

Vardeman-Winter et al. note that communication campaigns already made great strides in recognizing the potential of intersectionality in digital practices.[21] For example, organizations developing online platforms no longer require extensive background information (including binary gender information, race/ethnicity, and date of birth) before users can develop profiles.[22] Arguably, removing these demographic indicators can encourage participants who fear marginalization based on physical characteristics, thus aligning with the digital potential of intersectional spaces.[23] However, scholars call for more research examining how digital organizations integrate intersectionality into platform design to encourage users to contribute to the online space.[24]

Who Reads Reviews?

In a 2016 Pew study, 40 percent of Americans said they "always" or "almost always" seek out digital reviews before making a purchase decision.[25] An additional 42 percent said they "sometimes" look at reviews before making purchase decisions, meaning 82 percent of Americans turn to TPRS to make decisions on a somewhat-regular basis. Unsurprisingly, the highest percentage (53 percent) of young Americans (18–29 years old) report using TPRS always or almost always, likely reflecting the digital comfort and access of the group.

The same Pew study found that review-seeking behavior correlated with online shopping habits: "Overall, online shoppers are eight times more likely than those who never shop online to say they typically check online reviews before buying something for the first time (49% vs. 6%)."[26] Similarly, review videos, often produced by blogs or journalist/editorial teams, were more popular among young people, and more popular among women before making a purchase decision.

Since 2016, Pew's data demonstrates that using online reviews has increased by Americans. In a 2020 study from Pew, 93 percent report reading consumer reviews at least sometimes before making a purchase decision, 11 percent higher than the same study in 2016. Further, 81 percent of Americans report using TPRS as a part of their online research prior to making purchase decisions in 2020.[27] This greatly outweighed advice from family and friends (43 percent) and professional experts (31 percent). Digital reviews also greatly outweighed reviews from print media (8 percent) and religious wisdom (4 percent).

Overall, the number of Americans who turn to TPRS increased over the past five years, reinforcing the growth of organizations like Yelp and Google Reviews. However, alongside this growth, users also demonstrate a declining trust in the same platforms, which often means that they seek out additional information besides what they find on TPRS. While TPRS remain popular, most of Pew's interviewees add that sites like Yelp and Google Reviews are a "good place to start," but not the final authority on product or service reviews. For example, one participant reflected, "First, I will do a fairly rigorous web search, comparing multiple sources of information for both content and reliability. Afterward, I will follow up with books and other resources from the library."[28] Like many other participants, this individual reflects that digital sources, while still the first stop in research on purchase decisions, is not the final source of information. Twenty-first-century consumers are more likely to take a holistic view of information before making a purchase decision, rather than use TPRS without consulting other sources.

This is likely the result of declining trust in TPRS and criticism about the biased nature of reviews. The 2016 Pew study found that 51 percent of Americans thought that TPRS generally give an accurate picture of an organization, while 49 percent said it was "hard to tell if it's truthful or biased."[29] User criticisms largely critique the nature of reviews, often questioning the motives of contributors or the honesty of information. Despite the declining trust in the honesty of reviews, they are still listed as the number one source for consumer research prior to making purchase decisions.

Beyond differences between younger and older Americans and their use of TPRS, there are also differences between genders. Women are more likely to turn to TPRS and trust reviews, while men are more skeptical. This trend does not continue when looking at other forms of reviews, such as printed content (men and women equally trust print reviews in publications like *Consumer Reports*).

Why Do Users Trust Reviews?

While trust is clearly declining in TPRS, based on Pew's studies in 2016 and 2020, some of the initial reasons why trust was established early in TPRS popularity, remain. There are five reasons that users give for why TPRS are a trustworthy source of information: (1) the labor of contributors makes people question why someone would post a false review; (2) readers accept, and sometimes value, the "biases" of contributors; (3) users question if any type of information can be unbiased and completely trustworthy; (4) users recognize the efforts of TPRS to minimize false or fake reviews; and (5) TPRS are still easier to use than other forms of information collection.

These five reasons were identified from a series of in-depth interviews with Yelp users in 2019. The 30 interviews explored user rationale for using TPRS, issues of trust and credibility on sites like Yelp, and perceptions of the power of reviewing. Using a qualitative analysis, these five reflections on TPRS' trust are supported by quotes from participants.

First, the labor of contributors makes people question why someone would post a false review. Although most users recognize that entirely false reviews are present (most reflect that they come from paid professionals, such as "pay for review" businesses), the amount of work that is required to post a review makes readers trust most reviews they read. For one participant, recognizing that contributors are laboring without pay or direct benefit to create reviews made the information more valuable: "Sure, some might be paid for, but it takes too much work for all the reviews to be fake, no one has the money for that, so most of the reviews are trustworthy." Here, the user reflects that although he acknowledges some reviews are paid for by organizations, there are just too many of them to possibly all be fake, therefore making most of them trustworthy.

Similarly, other users reflected that it takes too much work for contributors to create fake reviews without a direct benefit: "Who has time for that? Unless some company is paying you to say something, no one has time to make up a good or bad review." Here, the user offers a common sentiment, that because reviewers do not directly benefit from their own reviews, there is little incentive to falsify reviews. Thus, most reviews are trustworthy, since there is little motivation for people to lie.

Second, readers accept, and sometimes value, the "biases" of contributors. There was also a common sentiment that reviews are inherently biased because they reflect one point of view and are not meant to be objective: "The whole point is to tell us about your personal experience, not some random fly-on-the-wall story about the company. I'm basically there for the bias." This reader, like others, reflects that bias in reviews is a critical part of the information-gathering process. Readers want to hear about individual experiences, therefore making the bias a normal part of TPRS. It is important to note that most users implied that bias was a threat to the trust of the sites, but a threat that was unwarranted: "I'm not sure why people worry if reviews are biased. Like isn't that the point?" It is unclear how users identified bias as the threat to trustworthiness. Was this a media narrative they replicated in discussions? Was this something they considered when evaluating each review? Was "bias" a stand-in term for paid reviews?

Despite these questions, participants not only recognized that bias was a natural part of TPRS, but actually of value to the reader:

Like if a company has done something bad enough to make you mad and post a bad review, I don't see how that's not valuable. Sure, it might not reflect everybody's experience, but the fact that you had a bad time, I still want to know.

For most participants, bias implied that the contributor was out for revenge or unfairly criticizing an organization. However, users seemed comfortable with the notion that these instances were few and far between: "Some reviews may be out of line, or like, totally the fault of the customer, but odds are that most of the reviews are a fair show of what really happened." Again, users did not feel that unfair reviews were prevalent enough to challenge the trustworthiness of the entire TPRS.

Third, users question if any type of information can be unbiased and completely trustworthy. For many users, reviews on TPRS were not the only form of biased opinions and information available when making purchasing decisions:

> If you can't trust Yelp, then you can't trust newspaper reviews of movies, you can't trust your cousin telling you what brand of pizza to buy, you can't trust social media people telling you what makeup is best. Bias is everywhere, everyone is biased.

From this reflection, identified biased reviews and recommendations across many media, not just on TPRS. Bias was an accepted part of consumer culture, which meant that TPRS had the same flaws as other forms of information and opinions.

Primarily, users offered advice on how to either embrace or avoid the bias of reviews. Many users added that reviews should be read holistically, not singularly. "You gotta read a bunch of reviews, you can't base it off one or two." Here, users suggested that the best way to combat the problems of bias was to look at a variety of sources, including multiple TPRS platforms. Information should be read as a larger set, not review by review.

Fourth, users recognize the efforts of TPRS to minimize false or fake reviews. For many users, Yelp's efforts to eliminate fake or false reviews and flag organizations who were found guilty of paying for reviews, was reassuring and demonstrated that the platform was working to become more trustworthy: "I'm not sure they caught them all, but it's nice to know that Yelp wants the reviews to be accurate and will delete fake ones." Here, although the user acknowledges that false or fake reviews may still exist, Yelp's efforts are helping make the platform more trustworthy.

Other users similarly identified the actions of the TPRS as helpful, yet incomplete in making the platform trustworthy: "They have a long way to go, but its in their best interest, and our best interest, to make sure fake reviews are gone." Again, there was widespread awareness and acceptance of the actions of Yelp to eliminate false reviews, which would enhance the credibility and trustworthiness of the site. Other users felt that TPRS could do more, such as verify reviews by following up with contributors, criminally pursue contributors who publish false reviews, or work with policymakers to establish laws or procedures that would help eliminate pay for review schemes.

Fifth, *interviewees suggested TPRS are still easier to use than other forms of information collection.* As users reflected on their use of TPRS, there was widespread acknowledgment of the weaknesses and problems associated with the site. However, these sites were still credited with being easier and more accessible than other forms of review information: "I'm not paying to see what someone else has to say before I buy something. Yelp is free, and I'm ok with a few glitches if the information is overall ok." For this user, free TPRS and reviews are better than paying for subscriptions to review publications or services. Because TPRS are free, users have more allowances for the problems described earlier.

Other users reflected on the accessibility of TPRS: "sometimes I don't want to wait before making a purchase. I just need fast information and don't have time for hours of research." The accessibility of TPRS on computers and phone apps makes users willing to look past problems of trustworthiness for the ease and speed of information.

In short, there are many reasons why users still trust TPRS for information when making product or service purchase decisions. It is not that users don't see problems with bias or pay-for-review accounts, but the benefits of these sites overcome the weaknesses and still make them valuable. As a result, TPRS are still powerful parts of the review economy, which can make or break organizations' profits and reputation. Despite evidence that consumer trust in TPRS is declining, the increase in the use of these sites also increases their power and position within organizational operations.

What Power Do Reviews Have?

Reviews can make or break a business, nonprofit, or organization. Just ask the nearly 4.9 million companies with pages on Yelp.[30] For these organizations, TPRS are often a scary, yet necessary part of getting customers, since the TPRS can increase the audience's awareness of an organization, but the organization lacks control over the messaging. This means that Yelp and other TPRS are powerful and uncontrollable publicity tools.

Within the interviews with Yelp users, many reflected on the perceived power that reviews can have, often citing personal examples of seeing businesses fail or succeed as a result (at least in part) of Yelp reviews. For users, Yelp presented three challenges for organizations: (1) organizations lack control of content on Yelp, (2) users are more likely to contribute to Yelp if they have a negative experience, and (3) information on Yelp is often unverified and inaccurate, therefore causing problems for both users and organizations.

First, participants were quick to reflect that organizations lacked control on Yelp because most of the content is generated by customers and reviewers. To participants, the only content controlled by organizations was the contact information on the very top of a profile and any responses the organization wanted to post to individual reviews. Beyond that, contributors and the Yelp platform controlled the information and messages: "Its probably pretty scary, you don't know what someone is going to post and you can't control it if you don't like it." For many users, the language of "control" was used frequently to illustrate an organization's ability to manage its own reputation. To participants, contributors controlled the reputation of an organization on Yelp, which therefore took the power away from the organization itself.

This language of control is critical to neoliberal public relations, in that the organization's control over messaging, publicity, and reputation is taken from brand managers and other traditional communication channels and given to the public. In this sense, the public now holds control over the reputation, thus challenging the traditional level of control experienced by organizations.

However, participants recognized ways that organizations could regain control, even given the limits of the Yelp platform: "I suppose they could put up some of their own reviews, or pay someone to write nice things about them. But, I don't think this happens as much as we think it does." Here, the participant reflects that organizations can turn to false or fake reviews to regain control over reputation on Yelp. This was a common recommendation from participants when asked how organizations can regain lost reputational control. However, as this participant also illustrated, many questioned if organizations would really adopt these practices, given that they are unethical and violate the terms and service agreements of Yelp (although no participants admitted to reading the terms and service agreements). Other participants agreed that even if there were organizations that regained control by using fake or false reviews, these organizations were limited to a small number, and users could probably tell by looking at the disparity between positive and negative reviews: "If you have a good or even ok rating, you're not going to pay someone to write a fake review. All you have to do is look at who use to have a bad rating, and then it dramatically changed. Anyone can tell that." Importantly, most participants assumed that users could easily tell organizations were paying or using false reviews. Further, the onus is on the user to tell, not the platform to weed out false or fake reviews. Many participants reflected that users must exhibit some media literacy skills when looking at reviews so that they are not prey to false or fake content.

Critically, most participants saw false or fake reviews as evidence of the power of Yelp. For many, the act of paying for fake reviews justified their perception that Yelp was a powerful means to influence or change the reputation of the organization: "Why else would they pay for it, you need good reviews on Yelp to get by. Maybe not the big-name stores, but if we haven't heard of you before, and you have bad reviews, you better fix that really fast." Here, the participant reflected that paying for reviews was a sign that reviews were a powerful part of the reputation of an organization, especially for smaller businesses with limited means to use more expensive publicity techniques such as commercials or advertisements.

Second, participants added that reviews could be problematic for organizations because people may be more likely to post if they have a negative experience, than a positive one. Many thought that reviews either skewed very positively (5 out of 5 stars) or very negatively (1 out of 5 stars). Participants perceived that average experiences were less likely to generate reviews, therefore skewing the reputation of an organization positively or negatively:

> Most people just want to vent on Yelp. They have a bad time and they want someone to hear about it. Maybe they want to warn other people, maybe they want the company to change, but either way, most reviewers are motivated when they have a bad time.

Venting frustrations was a common perception of participants. Many reflected that they thought very negative or very positive reviews were the most common, while average experiences were unlikely to solicit reviews at all.

For participants, the extremes of reviewing were a big challenge for both organizations and other users. For organizations, it could be hard to overcome a few bad reviews, since average experiences were unlikely to generate reviews at all. Therefore, the organization had to be excellent in order to overcome the negative content with better reviews. For users, it made it difficult to understand what a common, everyday experience would be like as a customer of the organization. Most participants acknowledged that very bad or very good experiences were abnormal, but without reviews representing the average experience, it would be difficult to make a true assessment of the organization: "Like how would I know what it would be like on a normal Tuesday. If everything is amazing or awful, what would my time be like?" For users, the extremes represented on Yelp made it difficult to picture a normal or regular experience.

It is important to note that the perception of extremes on Yelp does not reflect the true breakdown of positive and negative reviews on the platform. In December 2019, Yelp reported that 50 percent of reviews gave a 5-star rating, 18 percent gave a 4-star rating, 9 percent gave a 3-star rating, 7 percent gave a 2-star rating, and 17 percent gave a 1-star rating. This means it is way more likely that an organization receives a favorable review (68 percent receive 4 or 5 stars) than a negative one (24 percent gave 2 or 1 stars).[31] This challenges the public perception that many reviewers just want to "vent" frustrations over bad experiences. It is unclear why participants were so sure that negative reviews were more common than all other types, when statistically, they appear much less frequently. Regardless, participant warnings that negative reviews could hurt the reputation of an organization again reinforce the perception that Yelp is a powerful part of an organization's success and failure.

Finally, participants shared experiences when information on Yelp caused problems or difficulty for themselves and organizations. Many reflected that organizational profile information was frequently inaccurate, making it difficult to get into contact with an organization: "I did all this research, finally picked a painter, and then couldn't get a hold of them because the wrong number was listed on Yelp and the guy didn't have his own website." For many participants, Yelp is a means to identify, research, and then contact small businesses for needed services or products. However, many added that the contact information could be out of date or completely wrong. This was especially problematic for small businesses that did not have their own website or listing. This was also true of companies that went out of business (although Yelp does have a feature where users can note that a company is closed temporarily or permanently). For many users, the fact that it is Yelp users who create profiles for companies (not the companies themselves) was problematic, because the information could be incorrect or unverified by the actual organization: "Does Yelp reach out to companies once someone creates a page for them? It would help if they got verified by the company so that we know the info is correct." For participants, verified company profiles could help eliminate frustrations over faulty information or inaccurate contacts.

Neoliberal Public Relations

Based on the interviews with Yelp users, it was clear that participants both recognized the power of reviews, but also the challenges of trustworthiness on the TPRS. Grappling with issues of control, users understood TPRS as spaces where the public could impact organizational reputation, but also recognized that there were opportunities for organizations to (unethically) regain this lost control within the platforms.

Importantly, several participants invoked that their use of TPRS was a type of neoliberal labor, where they provided attention to Yelp in exchange for information that would help them make critical purchasing decisions. In addition, they recognized that Yelp needed the labor of contributors and users/readers in order to be profitable and successful as an organization.

Several participants also reflected on a specific type of contributor on Yelp, super reviewers, who provided verified reviews that appeared at the top of each organization's page. The Yelp Elite Squad (YES) was not only considered more powerful than regular contributors, but also a complicated part of the review economy because of their responsibilities on the platform and in organizational success. The following chapter investigates this group of reviewers to understand how they see themselves as a part of the review economy.

Notes

1 Carman, A. (2020, March 10). "Yelp says it shut down 550 user accounts after discovering a fraudulent review ring." *The Verge.* Retrieved from: www.theverge.com/2020/3/10/21171972/yelp-consumer-alerts-report-suspicious-reviews-fraud.
2 Segal, D. (2013, December 21). "A complaint registered, then expunged." *The New York Times.* Retrieved from: www.nytimes.com/2013/12/22/your-money/a-complaint-registered-then-expunged.html?ref=thehaggler&_r=0.
3 Angie's List. (2018–2020). "Reviews you can trust." *AngiesList.com.* Retrieved from: www.angieslist.com/faq/reviews-you-can-trust/.
4 Tyler, I. (2015). "Classificatory struggles: Class, culture and inequality in neoliberal times." *The Sociological Review,* 63(2), 493–511. Retrieved from: https://doi.org/10.1111/1467-954X.12296.
5 Tyler, I. (2015).

6 Gupta, H. (2016). "Taking action: The desiring subjects of neoliberal feminism in India." *Journal of International Women's Studies*, 17(1), 152–168.
7 Novak, A. N. (2016). *Media, Millennials, and politics: The coming of age of the next political generation*. New York: Lexington Books.
8 Novak, A. N. (2016).
9 Novak, A. N., & El-Burki, I. J. (2016). *Defining identity and the changing scope of culture in the digital age*. Hershey, PA: IGI Global.
10 Tyler, I. (2015).
11 Kosnick, K. (2015). "A clash of subcultures? Questioning Queer–Muslim antagonisms in the neoliberal city." *International Journal of Urban and Regional Research*, 39(4), 687–703. doi:10.1111/1468-2427.12261; Lelandais, G. E. (2014). "Space and identity in resistance against neoliberal urban planning in Turkey." *International Journal of Urban and Regional Research*, 38(5), 1785–1806. doi:10.1111/1468-2427.12154; Simon-Kumar, R. (2014). "Difference and diversity in Aotearoa/New Zealand: Post-neoliberal constructions of the ideal ethnic citizen." *Ethnicities*, 14(1), 136–159. doi:10.1177/1468796812466374.
12 Tyler, I. (2015).
13 Tyler, I. (2015).
14 Dy, A. M., Marlow, S., & Martin, L. (2017). "A web of opportunity or the same old story? Women digital entrepreneurs and intersectionality theory." *Human Relations*, 70(3), 286–311. doi:10.1177/0018726716650730.
15 Dy, A. M. et al. (2017); Leurs, K., Midden, E., & Ponzanesi, S. (2011). "Digital multiculturalism in the Netherlands: Religious, ethnic, and gender positioning by Moroccan-Dutch youth." *Religion and Gender*, 2(1), 150–175. doi:10.18352/rg.36.
16 McCormack, M., & Anderson, E. (2014). "Homohysteria: Definitions, context and intersectionality." *Sex Roles*, 71(3), 152–158. doi:10.1007/s11199-014-0401-9.
17 Okolosie, L. (2014). "Beyond 'talking' and 'owning' intersectionality." *Feminist Review*, 108(1), 90–96. doi:10.1057/fr.2014.14.
18 Trahan, A. (2010, 2011). "Qualitative research and intersectionality." *Critical Criminology*, 19(1), 1–14. doi:10.1007/s10612-010-9101-0.
19 Else-Quest, N., & Hyde, J. (2016). Intersectionality in quantitative psychological research: II. Methods and techniques. *Psychology of Women Quarterly*, 40(3), 319–336. Retrieved from: https://doi.org/10.1177/0361684316647953.
20 Else-Quest, N., & Hyde, J. (2016); Bilge, S. (2013). "Intersectionality undone: Saving intersectionality from feminist intersectionality studies." *Du Bois Review*, 10(2), 405–424. doi:10.1017/S1742058X13000283.
21 Vardeman-Winter, J., Tindall, N., & Jiang, H. (2013). "Intersectionality and publics: How exploring publics' multiple identities questions basic public relations concepts." *Public Relations Inquiry*, 2(3), 279–304. doi:10.1177/2046147X13491564.
22 Varderman-Winter, J. et al. (2013).

23 Bowleg, L. (2012). "The problem with the phrase *women and minorities*: Intersectionality – an important theoretical framework for public health." *American Journal of Public Health*, 102(7), 1267–1273. doi:10.2105/ AJPH.2012.300750.

24 Else-Quest, N., & Hyde, J. (2016); Varderman-Winter, J. et al. (2013).

25 Smith, A., & Anderson, M. (2016, December 19). "Online reviews." *Pew Research Center*. Retrieved from: www.pewresearch.org/internet/2016/12/ 19/online-reviews/.

26 Smith, A., & Anderson, M. (2016, December 19).

27 Turner, E., & Rainie, L. (2020, March 5). "Most Americans rely on their own research to make big decisions, and that often means online searches." *Pew Research Center*. Retrieved from: www.pewresearch.org/fact-tank/2020/03/ 05/most-americans-rely-on-their-own-research-to-make-big-decisions-and-that-often-means-online-searches/.

28 Turner, E., & Rainie, L. (2020, March 5).

29 Smith, A., & Anderson, M. (2016, December 19).

30 Smith, C. (2020, February 21). "80 interesting Yelp statistics and facts (2020) By the numbers." *DMR: Business Statistics*. Retrieved from: https:// expandedramblings.com/index.php/yelp-statistics/.

31 Yelp (2019, December 31). "An introduction to Yelp metrics as of December 31, 2019." *Yelp Newsroom*. Retrieved from: www.yelp-press.com/company/ fast-facts/default.aspx.

3 Yelp's Super Reviewers

With Julia C. Richmond, Ph. D.

In April 2017, *Forbes* magazine named the Yelp Elite Squad (YES) the most sought-after group of digital influences in the world, arguing that the community could single-handedly make or break a restaurant, business, nonprofit, or any other organization.[1] *Forbes* was not alone in this proclamation of the power of YES. *Business Insider, The Los Angeles Times*, and *Bon Appetit* magazine all summarized the success of this community by urging managers to take the group seriously or face the consequences of negative reviews. The articles profiled formerly famed restaurants that failed to appeal or respond to negative online reviews appearing in Yelp, Google Reviews, or OpenTable. In short, journalists were uniform in their analysis of the most elite digital reviewers:

> Consumer reviews are everything these days. It's the new currency, because everything happens on the palm of your hand nowadays, especially with the millennial money – everything happens on the phone. If they're walking down the street, they're going to Yelp and they're going to see what restaurants are rated the best on that block and that's how they're going to make their dining decision.[2]

Despite the clear journalistic conclusion that online reviewers and YES were paramount to success, few studies have explored this online community of "super reviewers," their relationship to TPRS and the digital review economy. Their relative power makes them important parts of comprehensive online strategy for public relations practitioners, and the exclusivity of their membership deems them worthy of scholars interested in the intersections of digital communities, promotional culture, and third-party credibility.

YES members are a type of "honesty broker," a term developed by Zukin to explain how users historically turned to trusted experts like

Good Housekeeping magazine when evaluating products before making a purchase decision.[3] Instead of journalistic credibility, YES members obtain credibility through verification by the Yelp platform and a rigorous application process that verifies their identity, autonomy from organizations, and honesty.

This chapter uses in-depth interviews to examine the motivations of YES members to better understand how the group operates, sees itself as part of the digital reputation management process, and articulates norms of membership. Largely, the results of in-depth interviews reflect congruity between the theory of neoliberal public relations and reflections on membership in YES.

The YES Program

Previous research notes the emergence of a digital elite group on most social media platforms, particularly ones where upvoting or other forms of promotion occur. Marland et al. note that elites are recognized by other users because of their trustworthiness and authority within the constraints of an online platform.[4] For Yelp, elites emerged because their posts were recognized for honesty, helpfulness, and accuracy.[5] While this pattern may emerge through structural elements, such as upvoting – more likely, elites are recognized informally by other users.[6] While elites do not need formal acknowledgment of their status, they do have more social capital and are thus more trusted on TPRS.[7]

Zhu et al. argue that Yelp's identification of elite reviewers, based on quality and quantity of reviews and involvement in the site, began in 2006.[8] At first, reviewers were nominated and upvoted by fellow users based on the helpfulness and perceived accuracy of reviews. Reviews with the most upvotes appeared at the top of an organization's page, thus becoming more visible to other users and reinforcing their popularity and impact. While structural, this mostly user-generated process identified elite reviewers through upvoting, with limited organizational structure provided by Yelp (i.e. the users were in control of elite positioning, not Yelp). The introduction of YES changed this recognition and removed control over status from the users. Instead, Yelp approved elite status after an application process against a set of organizationally approved standards. Askay and Gossett note that previous organizations (such as Facebook Leaders – a program now discontinued) that attempted a similar change in recognizing elite status faced outrage from non-elite members.[9] The formalization of this role changes power-dynamics within a digital space, particularly as it asserts organizational control in a previously user-dominated process.[10] However, because the

YES program was implemented early in Yelp's growth in popularity, it managed to avoid standard controversies and complaints. Still, formalization of elite status impacts how online communities behave, particularly in a review economy.

Chik and Vasquez note that the YES program changed how users responded to each other's posts.[11] Upvoting stopped completely, as top posts were now determined based on elite status, not user helpfulness. In addition, user responses to reviews (such as "thanks for the info" or "they took that off the menu") stopped. Chik and Vasquez propose this may be a result of non-elite members feeling disvalued by the system, although more research is needed on non-elite members before this conclusion is finalized.[12]

The YES Program started in 2006 following the success of in-person meetup social events created by Yelp in 2005.[13] The program offers members private events at new local businesses that are either free or low cost. These events are hosted by businesses with the goal to stimulate reviews on Yelp and boost online presence. YES events appeal to users because they are more exclusive and therefore less crowded than general events.[14] Yelp, along with local businesses, provide YES partygoers with special swag items during the event to further promote local brands.[15] YES reviewer parties are designed to connect users physically with others members with shared interests in local restaurants and attractions.[16]

Today, Yelp boasts nearly 8,000 YES members around the globe. Seventy-five percent of YES members live in the United States. To become part of the YES program, users must consistently post quality reviews and helpful photos while remaining socially active through upvotes and commenting.[17] To be considered for YES, users must be over 21, use their real identity (name, age, and location) on Yelp, and be nominated by other YES members. Yelp argues these requirements ensure that activity is regular, authentic, and fair to both users and businesses. However, membership is limited to select individuals and there are users who cannot join YES. Users are prohibited from joining YES if they own or are closely affiliated with a business. This stipulation includes communication professionals (PR practitioners) who manage a business site on Yelp.[18] YES membership recurs yearly and an annual re-nomination process is necessary for users to remain active.

YES members are demarcated online by badges on their profile and next to their names when posting. There are also special gold badges for five-year membership and black badges for ten-year membership.[19] While the YES program continues to be popular among avid Yelp users, small businesses and users filed four lawsuits against Yelp. One of the larger class action lawsuits claimed that Yelp exploited the work of elite members who created reviews without pay.[20] Yelp claimed the lawsuit was frivolous and it was later dismissed. However, lingering concerns regarding the credibility and standards of YES remain and are regularly voiced on protest sites such as YelpSucks.com.

Although Yelp regularly publicizes information about joining YES, few studies have explored membership from the perspective of YES users. Insight from this highly coveted group remains vital for practitioners as they attempt to attract YES members as well as scholars interested in TPRS and the review economy. In order to study YES member motivation for contributions to TPRS, this study uses a qualitative in-depth interview approach based upon the works of Karnieli-Miler, Strier and Pessach and Jeong.[21] Discourses are reported in the following section to illustrate the motivations, practices, and identities of YES membership. In total, five discourses were identified and are described in the following section. Twenty-three YES members were recruited and interviewed to understand how the group sees their role in the promotional mix and review economy. More information about the recruitment and interview process is found in the Appendix.

YES Interview Discourses

Discourse One: YES Reviews Help Shape Organizational Practices

Throughout all 23 interviews, participants reflected that they contributed to Yelp to provide critical feedback to organizations. This feedback would help change organizational practices and better future customer experiences. For example, consider this 24-year-old, female YES member from Chicago:

> When I go on Yelp, I'm making the world a better place. I tell companies what problems they have from a totally outsider point-of-view. It's hard for them to get this feedback from their own employees, so I'm the one that tells them what problems exist. Most of the time, good organizations make changes to fix the problem. So I'm making the world a better place – not for me, but for the next customer.

Quotes like this one illustrate that most YES participants were motivated by the opportunity to help organizations solve problems by bringing those problems to the attention of upper management. The participants saw themselves as part of the problem/solution process, often positioning themselves as the only people able to objectively tell a company what problems exist. For example, one 40-year-old male participant from Los Angeles added:

> My favorite review was of this chain in LA that had just awful customer service. They never got orders right, their employees didn't care, they weren't getting any better. So me and a few friends decided to post about it, and within days we got a response from management saying thank you and within a week, they had a whole new staff and things went a lot better. I'm sure the company had a lot of things to focus on, so they need us to point out problems so they know where to look and where to fix. Now, I'm not going back there because I remember how bad it was, but for other people, we made it better.

He went on to explain that his other complaints to a site manager at his local gym were unheeded for months, but as soon as he posted the experience to Yelp, he witnessed immediate solutions.

Other participants noted that Yelp acted as a type of "megaphone" for customers, thus empowering customer-driven change and problem solving for organizations. A participant expanded upon this by providing a hypothetical example:

> If you have a bad meal and complain to the chef, they might not do anything about it because you're one person. Even if you tell everyone you know, you're still a small group of people. Telling Yelp is like telling the world. It makes your voice so much louder. Chefs respond to Yelp because it's the largest group of people you could possibly tell.

All 23 interviewees provided a similar reflection on their motivation to participate in the Yelp community: to improve their own customer experiences through feedback that could make positive changes for all current and future customers.

While no participants directly mentioned "neoliberal" motivations of participation on TPRS, the consistent references to making the world a better place clearly reference the ontological view that these online reviews contribute to bettering organizational practices for all citizens, not just those involved on the site. In fact, many of the participants noted that, while their feedback may not directly impact their own experiences (due to moves or unwillingness to return to locations of bad service), they concluded that participating in the review culture would benefit them in the long-term. One 34-year-old male reviewer from Florida summarized this long-term effect by saying:

> I benefit all the time from other people's reviews on Yelp, and it would be pretty messed up if I didn't give something back. I'm contributing to the popularity of Yelp, and hopefully that will encourage somebody out there to post a review for something I can benefit from. In the long term, we all win.

Critical here, was that YES membership was almost always identified as a secondary motivation for participation on Yelp. As one 21-year-old female from Portland noted,

> I don't think anyone sets out on Yelp to become a YESer. Maybe because the whole program is not that old, but most people just want to contribute to Yelp, but they end up doing it so frequently or believe in it so much, they become YES members.

Participants commonly reflected that their YES membership was secondary to their real interest – building better organizational practices through customer feedback. Another 21-year-old female from Atlanta agreed, and added:

> YES is like a huge benefit for members, but I don't think it's the goal. You get to be a YES member only if you buy into the whole model of giving good feedback that can help other people make decisions and help companies improve.

For participants, YES membership was a perk of being tied to Yelp through shared belief in the power of feedback – not the primary goal or motivation of membership.

From this, public relations scholars and practitioners can identify a two-tiered set of motivations for participation in Yelp and YES. Primarily, participants felt that contributing to Yelp was its own type of reward that garnered improved customer relations and experiences, indirectly benefiting current and future customers. Secondarily was recognition from Yelp of individual members embodying the values and practices of Yelp culture. YES was viewed as a reward for participating in the site, not the primary force for participation. These two tiers are explored further in the coming sections.

Discourse Two: YES Members Create Communities
Based on Experience

Each of the 23 interviewees reflected that YES membership helped them build relationships with other reviewers within their region. For interviewees, YES membership was a way to meet other people with shared interests and a shared point of view on online reviews. As one 31-year-old male from Washington, DC reflected,

> when I moved [to DC] I didn't know anyone in the area. But because I was a YESer from New York City, I was almost instantly welcomed in the area by a group of people who wanted to experience the best of the city and believed we were helping make businesses better.

For participants, YES was a type of region-based community that provided a network of people who shared an appreciation for Yelp's purpose and mission to better customer experience for all.

The in-depth interviews revealed that experiential living was a motivation for individuals to join YES and participate in its events. For interviewees, experiential living meant trying new experiences, visiting new attractions, eating at new restaurants, and supporting new shops regularly. Experiential living was rooted in trying new things, rather than conforming to a routine. One 29-year-old YES female from Texas reflected on this experiential living,

> When I moved to Texas, I made a rule for myself that I would only eat at new restaurants for the first year. No repeats. I think that's what makes me a good YESer. I'm into experimenting and am open to trying new places.

Experiential living was a type of cultural norm for YES members, especially as they reflected on benefits of their membership. One 22-year-old male from the Pacific North-West added, "YES is all about trying new things and experiencing the best of Yelp. If you aren't into it, then don't join." Here, experiential living is not only the norm, but it is the boundary of membership.

For participants, formal membership in YES was different than the informal practices associated with being a YES member. For example, while new members are accepted into YES by regional managers appointed and employed by Yelp, many participants added that there were informal leaders of the group who acted as gatekeepers for the community. One 27-year-old male from New Jersey added,

> You might be accepted by Yelp into YES, but being a member is really more about getting recognized by the other YES members. And the only way to do that is to really adopt or show that you believe in experiential living.

Like other online communities, the informal membership rules and norms for YES demonstrate the ongoing desire of members to keep the communities insular and protected from individuals who may not prioritize experiential living. These are closed communities in two ways, both in the formal membership only recognized by Yelp's regional managers, and the informal membership that can only be recognized by existing members of YES.

This seemingly reinforces the elite label and status of YES members. Members must be accepted through two levels of gatekeeping – one formal, the other informal. Thus, YES members are identified as elite compared to regularly contributing members of Yelp. For three participants, this elite status complicated their relationship with the TPRS and caused internal dissonance. One 38-year-old male member from Hawaii reflected,

> I'm not sure I like the world 'elite' as part of YES. It seems weird that a site who wants to give a voice to people who wouldn't usually get to give feedback or help make changes, to suddenly say YES voices are superior or better than the rest.

Two other members also reflected that the elite status of YES complicated their relationship with the site and challenged their initial motivations for joining Yelp. For members who truly embodied the notion that the site gives voice to consumers who would otherwise be ignored, giving priority to some members through YES seemed counterproductive. After hearing this dissonance, researchers asked future interviewees how they rationalized or interpreted this status elevation of some members over others. One 39-year-old male from Florida summarized other interviewees' cognitions by saying "I don't see YES as a type of status, but more of a community of people who are recognized by Yelp as really wanting experiences. It's not about status, it's about commitment to the site and to experience." While more research is needed to understand how other, non-YES users interpret YES membership, these participants viewed YES as a type of experience-driven community.

*Discourse Three: YES Members Struggle to Balance
Experience and Credibility*

It was interviewees' love of new experiences that also provided a source
of cognitive struggle. YES members clearly stated they were a coveted
group of reviewers that organizations sought when designing events
and customer experiences. Interviewees discussed the numerous happy
hours, parties, trips, and sneak-previews they were invited to, simply
because of their YES membership. However, they also recognized that
these were no longer traditional customer experiences. One 25-year-old
member from upstate New York reflected,

> I joined Yelp because I wanted to give feedback on my daily
> shopping experiences. But now, the red carpet practically gets rolled
> out for me when I go shopping. I don't think my reviews are nearly
> as credible now because every experience I have is carefully crafted
> by some event guru who wants to really impress me.

Other participants similarly struggled with the authenticity of their
customer experiences, particularly as they compared them to their first
experiences reviewing on Yelp. Interviewees questioned if they were
getting authentic insight into customer experience. One 28-year-old
member from the Midwest added,

> When I show up somewhere as a YESer, I'm treated like royalty.
> But sometimes I wonder if it comes at the expense of other people?
> Like, because they pay so much attention to me, is there a table
> somewhere waiting for their food or having a bad time?

Interviewees questioned if their positive experience cost someone else;
clearly challenging their initial motivations for joining the site – to make
the world a better place for other people.

   Here, participants also questioned the credibility and insightfulness
of their reviews, particularly when Yelp highlighted them within the
platform. One 30-year-old male from Pittsburgh reflected on his time
attending a grand opening, exclusively for YES members, for a new
Chinese restaurant:

> It was the best opening ever and my review said that. But when
> I went a couple of weeks later, kinda undercover, the place was a
> mess. Bad service and food. So I went back online to add a new
> review. And now, there are my two reviews, one bad and one good

right at the top of the page because I'm a YES member. But which one is real? Which one should people trust?

It is the special treatment given to YES members that makes them question the credibility of their own experiences and reviews. For participants, the promoted status of their reviews (appearing top of each business page) does not reflect the quality of service or experience. Here, YES members question the insular nature of the community and its somewhat unknown purpose. One 28-year-old male reviewer from the Midwest added, "I think people trust YES reviews because they see it as 'verified by Yelp.' But really, our reviews can be less credible because we don't get the everyday experience. But people don't know that, so they trust us anyway." While most participants added that if users read about YES reviews, they probably would come to this conclusion, they also noted that most readers are not going to do that much work to verify the authenticity of the review.

For some YES participants, the carefully crafted events have helped them develop an ability to see through inauthentic displays of service. One 38-year-old male member from New England added, "I've got a way stronger BS-o-meter now because I've seen so many fake displays of customer service. Even when they do a bunch of stuff to make me love them, I can see right through it." While no consensus was reached by participants regarding the credibility of their reviews after carefully crafted experiences, it was clear that many YES members have at least reflected on the quality and authenticity of their reviews through this lens. This level of reflection was also applied to considering the power of YES membership, analyzed in the next discourse.

Discourse Four: YES Power and Responsibility

YES members positioned their participation in Yelp as both a responsibility and a reward for embodying Yelp practices and goals. For example, most participants reflected on review power in shaping a business outcome or success. One 22-year-old male from San Francisco noted,

> We went to a terrible grand opening at a spa a few months ago. Nothing was working properly – and they went through the trouble of designing the evening just for us. Now when we YESers went online that night to post reviews, it wasn't pretty. And they had just a one-star rating. I'm not saying we're the reason they went out of business, but I don't think anyone who read our reviews was eager to check them out.

Participants acknowledged that their reviews carried significant power and could potentially shut down an ill-performing business. This was partially a result of the site's organization and design. YES reviews appear near the top of the page and are typically the first reviews read by other users. New reviews, not crafted by YES members, appear below, meaning that even 50 positive reviews appear below one negative YES review. This hierarchy throughout the site suggests that YES reviews are more important or significant for users when making purchasing decisions. The weight of this responsibility seemingly weighed on ten participants. One 24-year-old female participant from New Mexico added,

> Like I think a lot about the power of my reviews. I don't want to be responsible for someone's business dying, but that's kinda what they can accomplish. So it really makes me think about if I should post my reviews. And now with the lawsuit stuff about bad reviews, I get even more worried.

Here, the participant notes that she, like others, thinks carefully about the power of reviews in the success of any business. For these participants, the power of YES reviews is a type of responsibility.

Importantly, four participants also raised the possibility of legal action around bad reviews. In 2016, a Texas couple was sued by a pet-grooming business for posting a bad, fake review. Since then, other businesses have taken legal action against bad reviews, especially ones with fake elements. For participants, the possibility of legal action was a new part of the reviewing economy and YES culture. One participant added,

> Would I say I'm scared of being sued for a bad review, not really. Most of those cases are about fake reviews anyway. But then again, what is fake these days? Can you sue me if you don't like my interpretation of your business? I used to think no, but maybe now I'm at risk because how many times I've posted bad reviews.

Other participants agreed with the new legal precedence set in the Texas case. If YES members are given power over the success of a business because of the positioning of their reviews, they could be at risk of legal action because of this power. One 21-year-old female from Portland added, "I want fake reviewers out of the site and sued just as bad as the next guy, they aren't helping anyone. But isn't it all just a matter of perspective?" For participants, help balancing reviewing power with the possibility of legal intervention was something they wanted from Yelp. These new and publicized court cases caused low levels of anxiety for reviews as they attempted to determine what they were and were not responsible for. Some even reflected they wanted legal aid from Yelp or promises of legal protections from the site in case of a lawsuit. While they were unable to give specific information as to what resources they wanted, it was clear this was an area of the YES and Yelp relationship that needed more attention in the future.

Discourse Five: YES Members and Public Relations

Lastly, participants reflected on their role in new public relations practices and digital relationship management. Interviewees saw themselves as a key part in new business management techniques, particularly as organizations evolve to stand out and provide customers with positive experiences. While the first discourse identified betterment of customer experience as a motivating factor in joining Yelp, YES was now identified as part of the public relations mix, a key component in modern, digital reputation management. Participants identified their contributions to Yelp as a part of new business models. This level of reflection, not just on how reviews impact customers, but also how they have changed and impacted the public relations field, demonstrates more holistic reflections on the power of reviews. One 38-year-old participant from Colorado added:

> before, if you wanted to know how to make your business better, you would have to hire some research firm and it could take months and lots of money. Now, you've got a hundred reviewers happy to help at any given moment – as long as you are willing to listen.

Participants viewed themselves as helping businesses succeed through low-cost and real-time problem/solution-based research. For participants, Yelp and YES was a vital part of the contemporary public relations mix.

For participants, the importance of TPRS was correlated to the willingness of businesses to listen to the feedback provided through the site. Participants shared many stories of businesses ignoring or challenging reviewer feedback. One 25-year-old male reviewer from the West shared a story of getting banned from a restaurant because of his review:

> The manager emailed me through my Yelp profile demanding I take down the review about his terrible restaurant. I told him that's

not how it worked and he should use what I said to improve the place. He told me I was banned and he would kick me out if I ever returned. I'm not sure if it's ego or something else that prevents people from listening to reviews. Like we're here to help you.

For some participants, getting feedback from managers or unhappy owners was normal after posting negative reviews. While YES members saw themselves as helping make businesses better, they acknowledged that not all businesses appreciated this feedback or integrated it into their business model.

Scholars and practitioners can garner valuable information from this last discourse, particularly as they design response strategies for digital reputation managers. Participants desired recognition for their part in new public relations practices without feeling managed or singularly identified.

Synthesis and Best Practices

While much more research is needed to generalize these conclusions to the larger community, the five discourses within this chapter identify the practices and motivations for joining Yelp and YES. Overall, participants demonstrated reflexivity as they considered the power and responsibility of the reviewing economy and their position within the digital space. While they lament individual public relations management, they demand recognition for their role in the contemporary digital public relations mix, particularly as they respond to a changing cultural and legal environment that may challenge the authenticity of reviews.

Overall, in-depth interviews with YES members highlighted five important discourses of membership motivation and practices. While generalizing these results to the whole of the YES community is outside the scope of this chapter, these qualitative insights provide several recommendations for practitioners and scholars seeking to define new digital reputation management practices.

Importantly, just like other reviewers, members of YES equally participate in neoliberal labor to TPRS that can be used by organizations or the platforms to reinforce or modify digital reputation. In fact, members of YES identify this as one of the aims of their participation and membership within the program. YES members wanted their reviews to impact the practices of the organizations they reviewed. They understood their reviews as a type of labor that could shape organizational success or reputation. For members of YES, neoliberal labor was not just a means to an end, but the point of their contributions.

Further, this neoliberal labor helped shape the community, something that YES members felt was a benefit of their contributions. By participating in the YES program, members were able to find other people, in their areas, who shared the passion of reviewing and the end-goal of making customer experiences better for everyone. This community-centric nature of YES highlights an important finding of TPRS: contributors view these sites as platforms for building community and even forming collective action that can modify or change organizational behavior to benefit the group. This community formation and collective action are critically important in the next chapter, as users turn to these spaces to advocate for policy or organizational change.

YES is a nuanced part of the review economy and formalizes a hierarchy of reviewers and the impact they can have on organizations and digital reputation. Not all reviews are created equal, and some, like those coming from YES members, have a much higher likelihood of impacting consumer decisions and organizational responses. While much more research is necessary to understand the full impact of YES and its members, it is likely that other TPRS will similarly adopt the structure of the YES program for their own platforms. This continually shifts how reviews are ranked or accessed by users when making purchasing decisions. As this process emerges, three best practices can help practitioners work with members of YES to fully embrace the neoliberal labor of the group.

Experiential Living and Events

For most participants, joining YES was a way to attend one-of-a kind experiences not available to regular users. Some of the best experiences provided by participants included: indoor skydiving at a new mall, being the first to test a new rollercoaster, behind the scenes cooking demonstrations, open bars, grand opening chef's tables, and first access to new designer wardrobes. While participants easily listed their favorite YES events, many also cautioned that these lavish events were atypical for most businesses, and therefore YES reviewers were more skeptical of the authenticity of such experiences. While they enjoyed these experiences, many said they would rather see a restaurant or shop on a "regular" night, while still getting a unique and positive experience. One participant summarized this by saying, "it's great you can put on a show, but I'd rather there was a cool experience every time I dine somewhere. We all want great experiences all the time, not just at YES events." For brand managers looking to develop stronger relationships with online reviewers, delivering experiential living on a daily basis was clearly in demand. One participant added, "I'd rather see you give everyone a cool experience, even if you highlight a few of those for me." For example, while the participant loved the indoor skydiving, he felt it should not just be brought to an event to impress the YES community. Experiential living is desired during all service interactions, not just for YES members.

Building Community and Networks

For participants, the most meaningful YES events were ones that capitalized on the sense of community and network that existed within the group. Participants wanted to mingle and talk with friends throughout the process, not just experience new opportunities. For example, one participant added,

> I went to a cooking demonstration that should have been awesome, but the chef didn't want us talking to each other because he found it distracting. They had the experience part down, but not the sense of community I want after leaving an event.

Because YES members meet regularly at these special events put on in their honor, it is important that events allow time for members to talk and socialize.

Addressing Reviews Holistically

Participants rejected manager's attempts to individually respond to negative customer experiences and instead favored more holistic approaches to addressing problems raised during reviews. YES members detested feeling managed and would rather see an organization solve problems instead of responding directly to the user. It is important to help YES members feel part of the public relations practice and to recognize their contributions rather than reject the feedback.

Overall, as YES membership grows and the group gains more presence in the twenty-first-century promotions mix, scholars and practitioners should pay attention to the neoliberal labor of the group and its role in the review economy. While the YES members evaluated in this chapter primarily focused their attention on local businesses, TPRS are increasingly used to review entities beyond traditional businesses. The next chapter looks at how advocates co-opt or use TPRS to form collective action and attempt to motivate policy or organizational behavior changes.

Notes

1 Wu, L. (2017, April 29). "10 lessons that restaurateurs can learn from Yelp." *Forbes.* Retrieved from: www.forbes.com/sites/lesliewu/2017/04/29/10-lessons-that-restaurateurs-can-learn-from-yelp-according-to-consultant-monti-carlo/#4062b4be330b.
2 Wu, L. (2017, April 29).
3 Zukin, S. (2004). *Point of purchase: How shopping changed the world.* New York: Routledge.
4 Marland, A., Lewis, J. P., & Flanagan, T. (2017). "Governance in the age of digital media and branding." *Governance,* 30(1), 125–141. doi:10.1111/gove.12194.
5 Schradie, J. (2011). "The digital production gap: The digital divide and web 2.0 collide." *Poetics,* 39(2), 145–168. doi:10.1016/j.poetic.2011.02.003.
6 Pearce, K. E., & Rice, R. E. (2017). "Somewhat separate and unequal: Digital divides, social networking sites, and capital-enhancing activities." *Social Media + Society,* 3(2). doi:10.1177/2056305117716272.
7 Marland et al. (2017).
8 Zhu, L., Yin, G., & He, W. (2014). "Is this opinion leader's review useful? Peripheral cues for online review helpfulness." *Journal of Electronic Commerce Research,* 15(4), 267–280.
9 Askay, D. A., & Gossett, L. (2015). "Concealing communities within the crowd: Hiding organizational identities and brokering member identifications of the Yelp Elite Squad." *Management Communication Quarterly,* 29(4), 616–641. doi:10.1177/0893318915597301.
10 Askay D. A., & Gossett, L. (2015).
11 Chik, A., & Vásquez, C. (2017). "A comparative multimodal analysis of restaurant reviews from two geographical contexts." *Visual Communication,* 16(1), 3–26. doi:10.1177/1470357216634005.
12 Chik, A., & Vásquez, C. (2017).
13 Harris, J. (2015). "For some Yelp reviewers, it pays to be elite." *Los Angeles Times.* Retrieved from: www.latimes.com/food/la-fo-0502-yelp-20150502-story.html.
14 Stone, M. (2014, August). "How to become a Yelp elite." *Business Insider.* Retrieved from: www.businessinsider.com/how-to-become-yelp-elite-2014-8.
15 Harris, J. (2015).
16 Stone, M. (2014, August).
17 Yelp Elite Squad. (2017). "About the Elite Squad." *Yelp.* Retrieved from: www.yelp.com/elite.
18 Yelp Elite Squad. (2017).
19 Harris, J. (2015).
20 D'Onfro, J. (2013). "Yelp reviewers sue the company because they think they're employees." *Business Insider.* Retrieved from: www.businessinsider.com/yelp-reviewers-sue-for-wages-2013-10.

21 Karnieli-Miller, O., Strier, R., & Pessach, L. (2008, 2009). "Power relations in qualitative research." *Qualitative Health Research*, 19(2), 279–289. doi:10.1177/1049732308329306; Jeong, J. (2011). "Practitioners' perceptions of their ethics in Korean global firms." *Public Relations Review*, 37(1), 99–102. doi:10.1016/j.pubrev.2010.09.004.

4   Scrubbing and Ethics

Considering the impact of negative reviews, it is understandable that businesses would want to regain some control over their digital reputations. How organizations try to control these spaces, however, falls into many different categories and holds ethical considerations. TPRS challenge the control that businesses have over reputation, messaging, and outreach to customers. Therefore, organizations often pursue means to regain control on these sites.

One of the most controversial practices, scrubbing, involves paying a TPRS for advertising space, in exchange for removing negative reviews. While the largest TPRS, Yelp and Google Reviews, claim to prohibit scrubbing on their sites, there is ample evidence shown throughout this chapter that scrubbing may still take place.[1] Many small businesses also claim that Yelp attempted to force them into scrubbing by promoting negative reviews until they paid for advertising. For example, Alia Meddeb, owner of Baraka Café in Cambridge, MA, claimed she was harassed repeatedly by Yelp sales representatives to buy expensive advertising content in exchange for keeping positive reviews on her page.[2] When she refused, Yelp deleted 450 positive reviews, claiming that because she changed addresses, those reviews were no longer valid.

Meddeb argues that because Yelp dramatically changed her online presence, her business suffered and her number of new customers declined rapidly. Because she chose not to engage in organizational control through scrubbing, she faced consequences. Not all small business owners feel strong enough to stand up to TPRS and refuse offers of scrubbing. Beverly Gordon, a small business owner in Toronto, felt pressured into buying $200 per month advertising content on Yelp, which claimed (or at least implied) it would help her ratings.[3]

There are other ways that organizations can regain control on TPRS and influence reviews and ratings. These options hold different ethical implications and considerations as businesses try to cope with the impact of positive and negative reviews.

How Organizations Can Control TPRS

Despite TPRS serving as neoliberal spaces that return the power of reputation to consumers, there are many opportunities for organizations to impact and exert control over online reviews. This can be done through official and site-approved means, as well as through covert means that violate the terms and service agreements of the TPRS. These include: (1) working with super reviewers to subvert negative reviews and replace them with positive ones, (2) paying for false or fake reviews, and (3) scrubbing negative reviews by paying the site to eliminate bad reviews in exchange for advertising dollars.

First, many organizations use super reviewers, like YES, to replace the reviews that appear first on their page with more favorable ones. As mentioned in the previous chapter, organizations court super reviewers with special events and treatment to elicit positive reviews. Because of the YES status, these reviews appear first on an organizations page and are generally more trusted than other reviews. While risky, organizations with negative reviews can perform well around YES reviewers, therefore earning positive reviews that appear first on the page. While this may not change a numerical average, it does improve the reviews that are most likely to be viewed by potential customers.

Second, organizations can pay for false or fake posts by offering individuals "reviews for pay." On the popular retail website Craigslist. com, there are dozens of advertisements for people willing to write fake reviews in exchange for money from an organization. These individuals are hired to write positive reviews without visiting or shopping with the business. Despite the availability of these services, these arrangements are considered unethical and violations of the terms of service agreements that individuals accept when creating a Yelp account. Because of the proliferation of these practices, Yelp now deploys anti-false or fake review practices by creating pop-up notifications that warn users when they visit an organization profile that was found guilty of paying for false or fake reviews. Additionally, Yelp expels accounts of individuals who accept money for reviews. Google Reviews, alternatively, leans on the public to identify false or fake reviews. Google asks users to "flag" reviews they believe are false or fake and decides after their own investigation. However, many organizational owners report that Google is slow to act and rarely removes posts even when there is ample evidence (such as if it is posted by a competitor).[4]

Third, organizations can turn to scrubbing, a controversial practice where organizations buy advertising content on TPRS in exchange for eliminating negative reviews. It is important to note that both Yelp and Google Reviews expressly forbid scrubbing as a practice and deny that they engage in such an activity. However, many interviews with small business owners around the country demonstrate that (at least at one point in time), Yelp actively promised eliminating negative reviews if small businesses bought advertising content on the site.

Scrubbing works because it gives the organization control over messaging in two ways. First, organizations can eliminate unfavorable messages within reviews. Second, they can purchase advertising space, and then control the messages within that advertisement. In total, control over organizational reputation is then in the hands of the organization, not the consumer. This is precisely why Yelp and Google expressly forbid it as a practice: it violates the neoliberal promises of their sites in which control is returned to consumer, not organizations.

While scrubbing and fake reviews violate the terms and service agreements of TPRS, there are other ways for organizations to turn negative reviews into positive opportunities. Organizations can employ digital dialogic communication practices, where, instead of trying to eliminate negative or bad reviews, they can engage the reviewer to learn more about the experience and adjust organizational behavior to eliminate or address problems. Digital dialogic communication asserts that organizations should take advantage of the feedback mechanisms of digital media and engage consumers for valuable insights into customer experience. By listening to customers, organizations can adapt practices that better serve their target audiences, therefore improving the likelihood of organizational success. While digital dialogic communication does not eliminate bad reviews, it does utilize reviews to improve business operations.

Despite the nearly twenty-year history of TPRS, there are still controversial practices with unknown legal and ethical implications and restrictions. Several examples from the 2010s demonstrate that the ethics of organizational control actions on TPRS remain unclear. By applying a set of ethical principles specifically designed for the digital era, actions related to organizational control can be evaluated.

15 Ethical Principles for TPRS

Bowen's work distills 15 ethical principles based on cases where organizations have pushed (and exceeded) the boundaries of digital communication. By examining controversial cases where there is confusion over ethical principles because of the newness of the digital frontier, Bowen clarifies the responsibilities of organizations, platform developers, and members of the public.

First, Bowen argues that organizations should "be fair and prudent" or "Consider fairness, justice, access. Consider right to know."[5] Organizations need to have "fair" intentions that require considering actions from both the customer and platform perspectives. If the expectation of the platform and users are that reviews accurately represent experiences and organizational quality, then engaging in scrubbing or fake reviews violates this ethical principle. The consideration of "access" is critical to this principle, in that it requires that all users have access to the information on TPRS. This calls for the TPRS themselves to ensure that users can access information in a fair way, which means using a "fair" algorithm for what reviews appear first on the page. According to Yelp, YES reviews are the "fair" ones to post at the top of organizational profiles because of the commitment by YES members to honesty and accuracy.

Second, organizations should "avoid deception" and consider "If it is deceptive, even arguably, simply do not do it."[6] Here, Bowen is clear that any action that could be deceptive or hide the truth from the public should be eliminated on TPRS. This includes the controversial practice of scrubbing. Importantly, Bowen does not invoke legal framework for deception, noting that there are many legal acts that are still deceptive (such as scrubbing). This principle also exists for users, who may be inclined to exaggerate experiences for dramatic effect when writing reviews.

Third, organizations should "maintain dignity and respect" of "the involved publics."[7] Here, TPRS need to consider how their platform helps or hurts organizations. When TPRS commit to working with organizations to ensure honesty and accuracy in reviews, they maintain dignity and respect. However, if they fail to work promptly to eliminate false reviews (even when identified by the organization itself) then, they both encourage deceptive practices and disrespect the dignity of the organization.

Fourth, TPRS should "eschew secrecy" by "barring trade/competition secrets" and carefully considering why information should be public. As of January 2020, Yelp and Google Reviews keep secret algorithms of what information is featured on their sites and what is buried deeper in organizational pages. Activist groups like "Yelp-Sucks" have called for an end to this secrecy so that organizations can better adjust to the platform and its impact on business success.

Fifth, TPRS should consider "if its reversible" or "How would you feel on the receiving end of the message? Is it still ethical then?" For

TPRS struggling to balance consumer neoliberal desires for increased control over organizational reputation and organizations' desires to maintain control of messaging, considering both sides of the argument will help.

Sixth, organizations and TPRS should be "transparent" and identify instances of paid speech. Currently, both Yelp and Google reviews do this by using the word "ad" next to sponsored posts or profiles. Similarly, organizations should be transparent when paying for fake reviews (although they are very unlikely to do so), in an effort to be transparent and trustworthy.

Seventh, individuals should "clearly identify" when speech represents the organization or just the individual. Organizations and users should recognize that most reviews represent one individual's perspective and experience, rather than being indicative of the entire quality of an organization.

Eighth, contributors should employ a "rational analysis" and "examine messages from all sides." When posting a review, contributors need to consider the impact of that review and its helpfulness to improving organizational practices. Rather than use the space to vent emotional frustrations, individual reviewers should aim for helpfulness to both the organization and the reviewer.

Ninth, TPRS should "emphasize clarity" by clearly demonstrating who authored posts and the context of those reviews. This is achieved by providing usernames, dates, and showing organizational feedback on all review posts.

Tenth, organizations should "disclose" all information that will help the audience with decision-making. TPRS, at the core, disclose critical information to the audience to help with purchasing decisions. Part of TPRS' appeal is that they provide more information than individuals previously had access to.

Eleventh, TPRS should work to "verify sources and data" and when necessary, eliminate reviews that do not uphold platform standards. This means that TPRS have a responsibility to verify if reviews are accurate and a responsibility to review challenges from organizations when a false or fake review is identified. It is unlikely that the platforms can individually assess each post and verify it. Instead, current systems encourage community members to flag posts that are suspected of unethical behavior, and then they are individually reviewed by the platform.

Twelfth, organizations need to "establish responsibility" and clearly demonstrate who is responsible for content reviews, verifying accuracy, and eliminating inaccurate or unethical content. Currently, there are differences in the approaches of establishing responsibility between

Yelp and Google. Yelp clearly articulates its own policies regarding scrubbing and fake reviews, placing the onus on themselves to pursue, investigate, and eliminate these practices. Google, however, clearly requests that users flag content and does not publicize its actions in eliminating these practices.

Thirteenth, "examine intentions" encourages users to reflect on their intentions when publishing reviews. If reviews are vengeful, exaggerated for effect, or unproductive (meaning they do not give enough information to the organization or the public), then they should be revised. Intentions should be consistent with the terms and service agreements of TPRS, in that they help other users identify and solicit businesses that fulfill a need. If a reviewer has an alternative intention, then they jeopardize the success of the site and its neoliberal intentions of serving the larger community.

Fourteenth, TPRS should "encourage the good" by rewarding reviews that are helpful for readers and the organization. Currently, Yelp employs "upvoting" where readers can assess the helpfulness of a review by giving it a "thumbs up" or "thumbs down." Reviews with more "thumbs up" assessments are considered more helpful to readers, and therefore appear closer to the top of an organization profile. Thumbs down reviews appear farther from the top and require more effort (scrolling) by the reader to access them. Similarly, Google asks "was this review helpful?" although it is unclear how this reader feedback contributes to the placement of reviews on a profile page.

And finally, fifteenth, TPRS and organizations should know that "consistency builds trust." As noted in Chapter 2, users look at reviews holistically, meaning that one single positive or negative review does not make or break the reputation of an organization. Instead, users look for consistency and repeated patterns or themes that emerge from many reviews over a period.

Based on Bowen's 15 ethical principles, TPRS, organizations, and users have responsibilities to act ethically when reviewing or engaging reviews. However, there are incidents that challenge the ability for these ethical principles to be implemented consistently. Two case studies illuminate the ways that these ethical principles are challenged by organizations and the TPRS, demonstrating the difficulty with adopting principles in an emerging and constantly changing digital landscape.

Neoliberal Ethics

In addition to the digital ethical standards that are articulated by Bowen, the neoliberal labor performed on TPRS is done with ethical expectations by contributors. TPRS' specific ethical expectations, articulated by contributors, shape the behaviors of users and the expected responses and developments from the platforms. Savin-Baden, Burden, and Taylor reflect that at the core of neoliberal labor are ethical expectations for how that labor is used on digital platforms.[8] Because neoliberal labor comes with an expectation for collective helpfulness, or the orientation that the labor will directly improve the consumer experience of other users and indirectly help the contributor, individuals who post reviews have expectations for how the product of their labor is used by a platform.

MacDougall adds that these ethical expectations vary from platform to platform and are impacted by a variety of other factors including prior experience, perceived industry norms, and personal ethical codes of conduct.[9] However, contributors are very unlikely to articulate these ethical expectations because they are innately woven into the performance of neoliberal labor. As a result, scholars must turn to case studies of instances where contributors feel that ethical norms are violated to understand the boundaries of TPRS and acceptable and unacceptable ethical choices on the platforms. The remainder of this chapter looks at case studies from Yelp to investigate how contributors respond to instances where ethical expectations are violated.

Cecil the Lion and Dr. Walter J. Palmer

During a June 2015 hunting trip to Zimbabwe, a Minnesota dentist suddenly became the center of one of the highest profile cases of scrubbing in Yelp's history. Dr. Walter J. Palmer visited Zimbabwe for a $50,000 guided-hunting lion trip near Hwange National Park, a protected animal sanctuary. During that trip, Palmer tracked and shot "Cecil the Lion," a well-known icon of the park and focus of a ten-year research project studying lion behavior. Palmer and his two guides argued that Cecil stepped outside of the protected park, thus making him available for the hunt.

Once Zimbabwe journalists reported Cecil's death, U.S. news quickly picked up the story and drew attention to Palmer's actions. Within days, Palmer was the feature of public outrage, most focusing on the ethics of his actions and the nature of planned animal hunts. Government leaders, including Minnesota Governor Mark Dayton called the hunt "appalling" and promised to investigate legal repercussions for his actions.[10] Celebrities and public figures like Jimmy Kimmel, Mia Farrow, and Jane Goodall took to social media to condemn Palmer.[11]

However, most of the outrage and direct confrontations came from members of the public. As the news story gained public attention, activist groups and enraged citizens mobilized a number of responses including spray painting the garage door of Palmer's Florida residence, leaving pickled pigs feet at his front door, and standing outside his Dentistry practice with protest signs.[12]

For outraged individuals without the means to travel to Florida or Minnesota, social media and Yelp provided a clear opportunity to voice dissent and criticize Palmer. As #CecilTheLion trended on Twitter, users threatened Palmer, released private details of his identity (address, age, digital media usernames), and links to the Yelp page of his Dentist practice, River Bluff Dental.[13] After Palmer deleted his personal and business Facebook and Twitter pages, users turned to one of the only online platforms that Palmer couldn't delete: Yelp. Within days, thousands of negative, one-star reviews appeared, primarily focusing on his hunting, rather than dentistry skills.[14]

Many of the reviews used humor and sarcasm to illustrate frustrations with hunting practices: "I needed a tooth extracted, so Dr. Palmer shot me in the neck with a crossbow, chased and tracked me for 40 hours" and "Brought my lion here for dentistry and was horrified by the result ... all kidding aside, I hope you die painfully." Other reviews adopted more threatening language, calling for punishment of Palmer and even threats of death.[15]

After two days, Yelp intervened on the page of River Bluff Dental and deleted all 7,600 reviews.[16] Yelp released the following statement to address outraged individuals after their posts were deleted:

> We, too, are horrified by the senseless death of Cecil the Lion and understand that many of us feel compelled to share our outrage. We are also equally committed to preserving the integrity of the review content on Yelp. This is why we follow the same approach for every business that lands in the news, good or bad, or even repugnant. And while that's a highly contested process this week, we are committed to keeping Yelp useful for everyone. We encourage you to continue the conversation on Yelp Talk.

For many users, Yelp's actions to delete their messages was a sign that the platform could intervene at any moment, making them suspicious that this practice was performed for other accounts even without controversial events. While Palmer did not pay Yelp, the company's actions drew attention to the content curation power of Yelp. Even though many users acknowledged the abnormal circumstances that forced Yelp to intervene on River Bluff Dental's page, they now suspected Yelp did the same for other pages, even without the controversy and public attention.[17]

Yelp termed the one-star reviews by angry users a type of "harassment" that violated the terms and service agreement of the platform.[18] Per that agreement, Yelp deletes thousands of "harassing" and "hate speech" posts from high-profile cases like River Bluff Dental and much smaller organizations.[19] However, Yelp acknowledged that it was unprepared for the high profile controversy surrounding its decision to delete user posts: "Yelp is working on it. 'We are learning as we go ... Nobody is prepared for that level of emotion and passion. And anger.'"[20]

While traditional scrubbing involves an exchange of payment from an organization in exchange for removing negative posts, Yelp's actions in this case constitute a type of scrubbing where an onslaught of negative posts motivates platform intervention. This scrubbing challenges the perception of public control on TPRS because it demonstrates how a platform can shape and curate the content by overriding users.

Yelp claims its reviewing platform is not an "activist space" and instead directs users to "Yelp Talk" to discuss controversial issues and events. However, activists and outraged members of the public frequently turn to Yelp because of the perception of neoliberal control. Users feel like they are the ones to control the content on an organization's page. So, when Yelp intervenes and challenges this control, it spurs outrage and frustrations with the platform, not just the organization.

Despite Yelp's clear authority and ability to scrub profiles (either for pay or in response to a terms and service agreement violation), some of Bowen's ethical principles are challenged by this response. First, scrubbing violates the claim to "maintain dignity and respect," because it fails to respect the opinions of reviewers. Although these opinions may be against the terms and service agreements, deleting them was clearly a disrespectful act, one that elicited frustration and outrage by many users.

Second, scrubbing violates "be transparent" because it fails to communicate (clearly) direct criteria for which posts can be scrubbed by Yelp, and which cannot. Although Yelp says that the criteria is set forth in the terms of service agreements that all parties sign when creating a Yelp account, these agreements are rarely read or understood by users. Therefore, these criteria need to be clearly articulated through another channel, but Yelp has failed to do so.

Despite these violations, there are also clear ways that Yelp's scrubbing of outraged posts also upholds several of Bowen's ethical principles. First, it upholds "examine intention" because it considers the harassing intentions of many of the contributors. Harassment violates the neoliberal intentions of the platform, which are to help organizations and users communicate and solicit feedback. Because these harassing intentions are counter to the design of the platform, scrubbing away these posts allows Yelp to uphold its value in the review economy.

Scrubbing also allows Yelp to implement a "rational analysis" and consider the situation from all sides. By considering how Palmer or River Bluff Dental may react to harassing posts, Yelp is empowered to scrub the profile for any posts that are about activities outside of dentistry.

Scrubbing remains a controversial practice on TPRS because different types may be classified as ethical or unethical. While paying for scrubbing clearly violates many of Bowen's ethical principles, scrubbing profiles for harassing and hate-speech-related contributions may be an ethical action.

San Francisco Small Businesses vs. Yelp

In 2014, a group of small business owners in San Francisco sued Yelp and accused the TPRS for pressuring them into buying advertisements in exchange for scrubbed profiles and positive reviews. After attending a local Chamber of Commerce meeting, several small businesses learned they were having similar difficulties with their Yelp pages. In an interview with business owner Nadia Kalnieva of S & Sons Moving Company: "she noticed a couple of negative reviews about her business were prominently featured. To make matters worse, she says, positive reviews about her company were hidden below in a 'not currently recommended' category."[21] Similarly, after realizing their good reviews were hidden while the bad reviews were prominently displayed, the owners started receiving calls from Yelp sales representatives who implied that purchasing advertising content on the site would result in scrubbed profiles: "What I got without spoken direct words is, 'Start paying, and we'll find a way to get rid of the bad reviews.'"[22]

Despite these implied offers, many of the small business owners felt they could not afford Yelp's advertising costs or did not want to run their businesses in a way that felt unethical. When the business owners refused to pay, they reflected that Yelp further hid positive reviews:

> Dloomy turned down the $350 a month advertising offer because he couldn't afford it. Then he says his situation only got worse: "What

I would notice is, I would get three to four positive [reviews] and a day later they would be gone, dumped in the hidden section."[23]

Despite several lawsuits from small business owners, many complaints to the Better Business Bureau, and even a lawsuit from stockholders who claimed Yelp misrepresented its business model, Yelp continued to deny these practices and claimed that scrubbing was unethical and not part of its model.[24] In an interview with CNBC, a Yelp spokesperson reflected, "There has never been any amount of money a business can pay Yelp to manipulate reviews and our automated recommendation software does not 'punish' businesses who don't advertise." However, the San Francisco lawsuit pressed on, refusing to take Yelp's offer to settle out of court.

A year later, the Ninth U.S. Circuit Court of Appeals in San Francisco ruled that Yelp was allowed to manipulate business ratings and profiles in exchange for advertising revenue.[25] Judge Marsha Berzon reflected, "'As Yelp has the right to charge for legitimate advertising services, the (alleged) threat of economic harm ... is, at most, hard bargaining,' and not extortion or unfair business practices."[26] For the owners, this was disappointing, especially because the courts found evidence of scrubbing, but did not view it as illegal or violating any laws. So, while the small business owners correctly identified that Yelp was promising scrubbed profiles for advertising revenue, the courts ruled this was a legal practice. Elgeko reflected, "In this case, the appeals court said the plaintiffs failed to show that the company violated their rights or broke any laws, even if they proved all their allegations."[27]

Yelp celebrated the ruling and used it as a way to respond to commenters and critics of its platform: "For years, fringe commentators have accused Yelp of altering business ratings for money ... Yelp has never done this, and individuals making such claims are either misinformed or, more typically, have an ax to grind."[28] Yelp failed to acknowledge that the judges did identify scrubbing on the site, and instead focused on the victory as justification for its messaging and practices.

It is unclear how many business owners have felt pressured by Yelp to pay for advertising in exchange for positive reviews (and how many have taken Yelp up on this offer), but Lawrence Murray reflected, "I've got hundreds of people who have called me with this problem: When they stopped advertising with Yelp, their good reviews got stripped out."[29] From these complaints, it is clear that scrubbing, where an organization pays the TPRS to eliminate negative reviews, is a practice used by some organizations.

Since this 2014 case, Yelp continues to verbalize a commitment to prevent scrubbing on the site. The site currently hosts a webpage about scrubbing and its actions against the practice, including pop-up windows on any company profile that claims to want to participate in scrubbing. It also shows evidence of a few companies who paid Yelp for advertising, but whose reviews and ratings remained constant.

Although there is ample evidence that Yelp, at least at some point in time, engaged in scrubbing behaviors, the company maintains it is an unethical practice and claims that organizations cannot pay for better reviews. It also argues that there are other ways that organizations can improve their ratings, such as using the feedback to improve business practices that will enhance customer experiences. Essentially, Yelp suggests businesses use digital dialogic communication as an ethical alternative to better their organizations and improve ratings.

Digital Dialogic Communication as a Practice

Established in the later 1990s, digital dialogic communication emerged as a body of theory and practices to help organizations maximize the potential of new online digital spaces.[30] In particular, the theory encouraged organizations to use online feedback solicited on message boards and blogs to improve business practices to better fit the needs and desires of the audience.[31] Organizations were encouraged to listen to the public, ask questions, and respond to inquiries, all using digital media.[32] In doing so, organizations would adopt mutual adjustment practices where feedback could be used to inform organizational changes. Further, by communicating these changes back to the public, the audience could also adjust its perception and opinion of the organization to account for the new information.

At the heart of digital dialogic communication is "dialogue" or the concept of open communication between entities that actively listen and respond to each other, then adjust perceptions and behaviors according to the information exchanged.[33] This dialogue also produces a relationship between the organization and the audience, meaning that by soliciting feedback, engaging in dialogue, and performing mutual adjustment, a stronger relationship develops.[34] As a result, digital dialogic communication is not just a means to improve business practices, but also a way to strengthen relationships between an organization and its customers.

TPRS provide an ideal space for digital dialogic communication because of the feedback mechanism that is structurally in place.

Feedback is invited on TPRS, which can then be used as a catalyst for communication between the organization and a contributor. Sites like Yelp and Google Reviews allow organizations to post responses to each review, which can cultivate conversation and discussion, or dialogue. This dialogue can then be used to inform business practice adjustments, as well as adjustments to how the user perceives the organization.

Digital dialogic communication is an ethical alternative to scrubbing and false and fake reviews. It upholds several of Bowen's ethical principles including "avoid deception," "be transparent," "disclose," and "establish responsibility." Because dialogue is transparent and easily visible to all who search the page, there is evidence that the organization takes reviews seriously and uses them to improve the organization for the good of customers (by adjusting to consumer feedback and needs). Rather than delete negative reviews through unethical scrubbing means, by ethically engaging the customer in dialogue, negative reviews are an opportunity to demonstrate a commitment to the public.

Digital dialogic communication, however, is not a guarantee of fixing reputational problems that emerge from negative reviews. First, it requires organizational leaders to monitor and devote time to communicating with contributors. For many small business owners, the investment of time is problematic, especially when balancing other ownership responsibilities. Second, even if the organization has enough time to devote to building dialogue, the skills involved in doing so may be outside the abilities of organizational leaders. This type of communication takes patience, empathy, and the ability to communicate clearly and positively, even when faced with emotional or frustrated consumers. Maintaining this tone is critical to building successful dialogue, but difficult for inexperienced or untrained communicators.

Third, the organization must "buy into" the value of dialogue and the feedback solicited on TPRS. Feedback must be used, and organization change must be demonstrated (not just promised). For many organizational leaders, it can be tempting to discredit negative reviews and ignore the feedback provided on TPRS. However, in order to maximize the potential of dialogue, organizations must be committed to making changes based on this feedback.

Fourth, contributors must also "buy into" the dialogue process and continue to communicate after the initial post. Dialogue involves both parties committed to feedback and mutual adjustment. Therefore, the contributor must be committed to answering further questions and listening to information from the organization (potentially about business practice changes based on the dialogue).

Finally, the value of this dialogue emerging on TPRS is that it is visible to those who are not directly involved. This means that other users can witness the information exchange between a contributor and organization, and then use that information to adapt their own perceptions. However, many users do not go far enough into each organizational profile to look at emerging conversations based on a single review. A quick skim of a page may prevent a user from seeing the digital dialogic communication and appreciating its value. Further, digital dialogic communication may take place offline. Many organizations refer contributors of negative reviews to customer service or other channels of communication. If digital dialogic communication takes place outside of a site, it is invisible to outside users.

It is likely that many organizations prefer the more unethical approaches of scrubbing or paying for fake reviews because they require less effort and time investment than true digital dialogic communication. However, if organizations want to embrace the neoliberal potential of TPRS and respect the control that TPRS give to consumers, digital dialogic communication is the best means to adapt organizational practices and use the site.

There are also instances where digital dialogic communication may not be sufficient to deal with negative reviews. There are legal approaches that organizations can use to respond to reviews that are problematic. While they may not have the positive impact of digital dialogic communication at enhancing business practices to better meet customer needs, they fulfill the need of organizations to protect their digital reputations and combat negative reviews.

Notes

1 Lutz, A. (2013, April 25). "Restaurant manager says Yelp is killing his business." *Business Insider.* Retrieved from: www.businessinsider.com/owner-yelp-is-bad-for-small-business-2013-4.

2 Keller, A. (2017, August 23). "For Yelp, extortion has a starring role." *The Technoskeptic.* Retrieved from: https://thetechnoskeptic.com/yelp-extortion-starring-role/.

3 Harris, S. (2014, January 17). "Yelp accused of bullying businesses into paying for better reviews." *CBC-Radio Canada.* Retrieved from: www.cbc.ca/news/business/yelp-accused-of-bullying-businesses-into-paying-for-better-reviews-1.2899308.

4 Wai, S. (2019, January 14). "How to deal with or remove fake negative Google reviews." *Tribute Media.* Retrieved from: www.tributemedia.com/blog/how-to-deal-with-or-remove-fake-negative-google-reviews.

5 Bowen, S. (2013). "Using classic social media cases to distill ethical guidelines for digital engagement." *Journal of Mass Media Ethics*, 28(2), 119–133. Retrieved from: https://doi.org/10.1080/08900523.2013.793523.

6 Bowen, S. (2013).

7 Bowen, S. (2013).

8 Savin-Baden, M., Burden, D., & Taylor, H. (2017). "The ethics and impact of digital immortality." *Knowledge Cultures*, 5(2), 178–196. Retrieved from: https://doi.org/10.22381/KC52201711.

9 MacDougall, R. (2010). "eBay ethics: Simulating civility today, for the "digital democracies" of tomorrow." *Convergence*, 16(2), 235–244. Retrieved from: https://doi.org/10.1177/1354856509357584.

10 CBS Minnesota. (2015, July 29). "Politicians speak out on the death of Cecil the Lion." *CBS Minnesota*. Retrieved from: https://minnesota.cbslocal. com/2015/07/29/politicians-speak-out-on-the-death-of-cecil-the-lion/.

11 Leeds, S. (2015, July 29). "Jimmy Kimmel speaks out on the killing of Cecil the Lion." *The Verge*. Retrieved from: https://blogs.wsj.com/speakeasy/2015/07/29/jimmy-kimmel-speaks-out-on-the-killing-of-cecil-the-lion/ ?mod=e2fb.

12 Dockterman, E. (2015, July 29). "Dentist who killed Cecil the Lion writes letter apologizing to his patients." *Time*. Retrieved from: https://time.com/ 3977018/cecil-lion-walter-palmer-letter/.

13 RT Staff. (2015, July 28). "The hunting of Walter Palmer: Internet goes after 'lion killer' US dentist." *RT*. Retrieved from: www.rt.com/usa/311002-dentist-lion-internet-hunt/.

14 Toor, A. (2015, July 29). "Yelp reviewers tear apart American dentist who killed Cecil the lion." *The Verge*. Retrieved from: www.theverge.com/2015/ 7/29/9065981/cecil-the-lion-killed-walter-james-palmer-dentist-yelp-review.

15 Toor, A. (2015, July 29).

16 Rietmulder, M. (2015, September 30). "The only honest Yelp review of River Bluff Dental, home of the lion killer." *City Pages*. Retrieved from: www.citypages.com/news/the-only-honest-yelp-review-of-river-bluff-dental-home-of-the-lion-killer-7708161.

17 Dewy, C. (2015, July 28). "A vengeful Internet trashed the Yelp page of the Minnesota dentist who shot Cecil the lion." *The Washington Post*. Retrieved from: www.washingtonpost.com/news/the-intersect/wp/2015/ 07/28/a-vengeful-internet-trashed-the-yelp-page-of-the-minnesota-dentist-who-shot-cecil-the-lion/.

18 Lately, D. (2015, August 21). "A one-star human being: The strange, unwilling role Yelp plays in Internet shaming." *Slate*. Retrieved from: https://slate.com/technology/2015/08/lion-killing-dentist-walter-palmers-yelp-page-and-the-business-of-internet-shaming.html.

19 Lately, D. (2015, August 21).

20 Lately, D. (2015, August 21).

21 Harris, S. (2014, January 17).

22 Harris, S. (2014, January 17).

23 Harris, S. (2014, January 17).

24 Harris, S. (2014, January 17).
25 Egelko, B. (2014, September 4). "Yelp can manipulate ratings, court rules." *San Francisco Gate.* Retrieved from: www.sfgate.com/news/article/Yelp-can-give-paying-clients-better-ratings-5731200.php.
26 Egelko, B. (2014, September 4).
27 Egelko, B. (2014, September 4).
28 Egelko, B. (2014, September 4).
29 Egelko, B. (2014, September 4).
30 Sommerfeldt, E., & Yang, A. (2018). "Notes on a dialogue: Twenty years of digital dialogic communication research in public relations." *Journal of Public Relations Research,* 30(3), 59–64. Retrieved from: https://doi.org/10.1080/1062726X.2018.1498248.
31 Men, L., Tsai, W., Chen, Z., & Ji, Y. (2018). "Social presence and digital dialogic communication: Engagement lessons from top social CEOs." *Journal of Public Relations Research,* 30(3), 83–99. Retrieved from: https://doi.org/10.1080/1062726X.2018.1498341.
32 Morehouse, J., & Saffer, A. (2018). "A bibliometric analysis of dialogue and digital dialogic research: Mapping the knowledge construction and invisible colleges in public relations research." *Journal of Public Relations Research,* 30(3), 65–82. Retrieved from: https://doi.org/10.1080/1062726X.2018.1498343.
33 Kent, M. L., & Taylor, M. (1998). "Building dialogic relationships through the World Wide Web." *Public Relations Review,* 24(3), 321–334.
34 Shin, W., Pang, A., & Kim, H. J. (2015). "Building relationships through Integrated Online Media: Global organizations' use of brand web sites, Facebook, and Twitter." *Journal of Business and Technical Communication,* 29(2), 184–220.

5   Lawsuits and Organizational Control

After months of an exhausting court battle between a wedding photographer and her former clients, Andrea Polito came out victorious. Polito sued newlyweds Neely and Andrew Moldovan for defamation after the couple mounted an intensive digital campaign designed to hurt her photography business. The couple, married just one year before, was unhappy because of a $125 charge for a cover photo for their wedding album. After weeks of arguing over the fee, which was explained in the contract signed by the couple prior to the wedding, Polito was ready to give in and pay for the charge herself. That was when she became aware of the Moldovans' attempts to hurt her reputation through traditional news interviews and negative posts on TPRS like Wedding Wire. In the wedding and special events industries, Wedding Wire, The Knot, and Zola are essential tools to connect brides and grooms with professionals, such as photographers. Negative reviews on these sites can be extremely costly, as Polito quickly found out.

As organizations and customers grapple for control over digital reputations and messaging, lawsuits like Polito's grow more common, accusing dissatisfied customers of libel and defamation based on the impact of negative (often false) reviews on TPRS. Organizations, that lack the control to edit or modify reviews on TPRS, may need legal intervention to prevent significant damages to their business and livelihood. As these lawsuits appear (and become successful), consumer activist groups caution that customers are fearful of being sued for posting content that a retailer would find dissatisfying. TPRS' leadership have also vocalized concerns over the legal practice of suing contributors, worrying that this practice may make it less likely for someone to post a review at all.

However, for business owners like Polito, sometimes the legal system is necessary to rectify problems associated with negative reviews. When scrubbing and digital dialogic communication is not enough, and there is evidence that the contributors posted with malicious and untruthful intent, the courts have now demonstrated their willingness to intervene. Despite the court's participation and clear legal rulings regarding defamation on TPRS, these actions are controversial and often elicit mixed reactions from the public and TPRS users. This begs the questions, "are defamation lawsuits doing more harm than good in rectifying the damages associated with negative reviews?" and, "what is the effect of defamation lawsuits on the neoliberal assumptions of users engaging in TPRS?"

Polito vs. the Moldovans

Nancy Polito ran one of the most successful wedding photography businesses in Dallas before she was hired for the Moldovans' wedding in 2015. With a photography studio on the well-known North Market Street, Polito was hired for several million-dollar weddings of Dallas elites, booking anywhere from 75 to 100 weddings each year. However, after fighting with the Moldovans because of the $125 album cover charge, Polito said her business was "destroyed."[1]

The Moldovans launched an impressive campaign against Polito, arguing the $125 charge was unjustified. They took their message to local news channels such as NBC5, arguing Polito was "holding their photos hostage."[2] Beyond television news, the Moldovans also turned to TPRS, specifically Polito's pages on Wedding Wire and Google Reviews. There, the couple posted fake negative reviews under aliases and liked other negative posts (especially ones that were clearly hyperbolic or fake, such as one that accused Polito of giving a customer AIDS).

With that, Polito said the Moldovans ruined the reputation of her 13-year-old business "almost overnight."[3] She said in the following year, she only booked two weddings, a significant decline from her normal 75 to 100. Although Yelp intervened and removed some of the fake reviews posted by the Moldovans, other TPRS were reluctant, and the negative reviews remained. Polito said the damage was permanent because of the variety of channels used by the couple.

The following March, Polito filed a civil suit against the Moldovans to pursue damages for defamation. After several months, a Dallas jury awarded Polito $108 million in damages, agreeing that the Moldovans had acted maliciously and lied about Polito's services and actions. The Dallas couple reflected they were "stunned" by the outcome:

> We were unhappy with a situation, so we complained like anyone would. This court decision tells consumers not to speak up for fear

of fat legal bills and painful judgements … If this is the cost of standing up for what's right, we should have given in to start with. But we hope to prevail in the end.

Years later, the Moldovans have not filed for an appeal.

Polito's case was widely covered because it served as a prime example of how organizations could regain control over negative reviewers and because it played to the anxiety of site users regarding their own liability. When looking at the comments section of news articles about the lawsuits, this dueling perspective is highly evident.

First, there are clearly readers who sympathize with Polito's position and experience. For example,

> Good verdict. Smart jury. It's about time that these maggots got what they deserve. They started early in the process by stiffing the photographer on the first $125. Then the defamation and loss of business from a crusade by an obviously mentally ill POS is going to cost the deadbeats bigly. This kind of slime will file bankruptcy to avoid the just outcome of the lawsuit. But at least the photog will be vindicated somewhat.[4]

Here, the reader reflects that they believe the photographer was in the right by maliciously describing the Moldovans. Other readers similarly accused the Moldovans of unethical behavior, mental illness, and called them names. This was the most common response by readers, many vocalizing sympathies for Polito's lost reputation and business.

Other readers vocalized support for Polito because they, too, felt attacked by fake or exaggerated negative reviews that hurt their businesses to bring attention to, or interest in, the Moldovans and their lifestyle blogs:

> I'm a venue sales director in a major US city and have dealt with all kinds of social event bookings incl weddings, corporate events and so on. It's simply astounding the number of clients that actually read their contract. Hardly anyone does. The time to negotiate is BEFORE you sign, the time to ask questions is BEFORE you sign, the time to making additional requests is BEFORE you sign … Of course in this scenario the client went way off track & the whole thing turned bully/gang up, which never results in a good outcome for anyone. I'm happy that Andrea was able to be vindicated & think it's pretty terrible that the client has so far chosen to not use this as a "teaching moment" on her "lifestyle" blog. Apparently

that lifestyle doesn't include humility or the ability to reflect on the past with honesty.[5]

Others, however, criticized Polito's actions, arguing that her lawsuit did more harm than good because it publicized the negative reviews even more and made her look like she was vengeful: "First time someone actually gets sued and the story makes rounds on the web, it'll be a backlash like no other ... the photog would almost certainly get more bad press then support. Bad idea."[6] Others agreed that the lawsuit could do more harm than good and challenged Polito's argument that she was trying to make up for the damages caused to her business. Several readers questioned why Polito would want to draw more negative attention to her brand, saying the lawsuit undermined her pleas to the jury to recoup lost damages: "Whatever happens, justified or not, I imagine suing clients is likely to blow up in your face."[7]

Other readers reflected that lawsuits like Polito's symbolize the difficulty we have with understanding the relationship between modern day organizations and consumers:

> The thing about social media is that we are all responsible for our own words and posts. If we celebrate that an individual can be empowered to take a legitimate issue, elevate it in social media and gain power against businesses, I'd suggest we also have to celebrate when those businesses avail themselves of legal means to fight back when those actions are slanderous, incorrect and illegal.[8]

For this reader, Polito's lawsuit should be celebrated because it helps organizations provide more truthful information, all while acknowledging that sometimes the control given by TPRS to users can be manipulated or misused.

For many readers, Polito's lawsuit produced anxiety over the nature of defamation, slander, and libel, especially on TPRS. Many readers considered their own reviews and wondered if they could face similar legal repercussions for their posts. While most also hedged these concerns by acknowledging the Moldovans took their reviews to an extremely vengeful and unethical place, they also were concerned that lawsuits could become more normalized as a way for organizations to enact revenge on unhappy reviewers: "I hope to see more updates on how the court handles these types of conflicts, as I'm sure that more service providers will (or attempt to) manage unhappy customers."[9] And, "Online reviews are worthless anyway. Half the posters love them, half the posters hate them. Now it seems only positive posts are allowed."[10]

Although Polito's case was settled at the end of 2015, newer lawsuits regarding TPRS have failed to gain this type of attention and critical reception. Perhaps it was the novelty of Polito's case, or the ability of readers to sympathize with both Polito's and the Moldovans' perspectives. Either way, the case raises anxiety over what type of reviews can elicit lawsuits, what type of speech is protected in TPRS, and what the impact of these lawsuits may have on contributors' willingness to review organizations.

Can You be Sued for a Fake Review?

In short, yes. Although it is very rare, organizations can sue for defamation, libel, or slander, depending on their state laws. Texas defines defamation as "false and unprivileged publication, which exposes any person to hatred, contempt, ridicule, or obloquy, or which causes the same to be shunned or avoided, or which tends to injure him in his occupation."[11] Defamation can come in two forms, libel or slander. Libel is written defamation defined by fixed documentation such as text, picture, graphic, or effigy. Slander is spoken or oral, and it may be communicated in-person or through radio. In lawsuits involving TPRS, most organizations sue for damages related to libel defamation, because the act of publishing a review online constitutes fixed documentation.

Defamation is one of the most difficult legal arguments to prove because, depending on the state, there are various criteria that need to be met. First, the plaintiff (the organization) must prove that the contributor provided knowingly false information. That means, the contributor lied, and the organization has evidence that they had accurate information that was willingly ignored or manipulated. Second, the plaintiff must prove that the contributor had malicious intent and sought to cause damage to the reputation of the organization. Third, the plaintiff must prove that damage occurred, resulting in monetary loss, such as loss of profits or revenue. Other states have additional requirements, such as a statute of limitations that defines a window of time where a lawsuit can take place.

Defamation, while difficult to prove under normal circumstances, can be even more complicated for organizations in the digital space. One challenge is identifying the speaker or author of posts. While Yelp's terms and conditions require users to provide accurate contact information, usernames are frequently creative and do not use the full name of the contributor. That makes identifying the speaker difficult, therefore making it difficult for plaintiffs to prove they are suing the correct person. Additionally, archiving posts is critically important to establishing a timeline in defamation cases. Users can delete their own posts or modify existing posts. So, if an organization has not archived or documented the defamation completely, they will not have access to past posts via the TPRS.

Defamation lawsuits about reviews on TPRS also have a history of failure. Tom Lloyd was sued for $25,000 by DeLand Animal Hospital and veterinarian Thomas MacPhail for a one-star review. Lloyd posted that his 10-year-old dog died while waiting for surgical care at the hospital. Weeks later, he was sued for his review because the hospital claimed it was false information designed to malign the reputation of the veterinarian.[12] Lloyd successfully defended his case and a Florida judge dismissed the hospital's claims after two veterinarians testified to the accuracy of the review.[13] However, in defending himself, Lloyd accrued legal bills of $26,000, more expensive than the initial lawsuit and his $20,000 social security annual income: "I'm finding out that isn't always cheap to give an honest review, because if the other person has money, they can drive you in the ground."[14]

Importantly, even Yelp suggests that states like New York need stronger consumer protection measures to ensure that contributors are comfortable posting reviews.[15] In addition, Yelp encourages businesses to settle issues with reviewers individually and without legal interventions. In the past, Yelp has remained neutral in these lawsuits, choosing to provide minimum information (such as user information) to plaintiffs unless mandated by the courts.[16]

The Public Participation Project, an organization dedicated to protecting free speech online, argues that most lawsuits about site reviews are SLAPPs (Strategic Lawsuit Against Public Participation), designed to intimidate the current contributor and future contributors rather than specifically address defamation or prove a case.[17] In these cases, SLAPPs aim to threaten the contributor into erasing or eliminating a previous post because of the extensive legal costs of fighting a lawsuit. Some states have started creating anti-SLAPP legislation that punishes organizations or individuals who use lawsuits and court resources to intimidate members of the public. However, not all states hold these policies, and not all states recognize SLAPP as it applies to digital communication.

It is also difficult to differentiate SLAPPs from legitimate claims of defamation. Many organizations feel pressured to use the legal system because they feel as if they have no other options to combat negative reviews. The neoliberal power given to individuals by TPRS can be difficult to reconcile, and for organizations with the resources, SLAPPs can help intimidate critics and prevent future negative reviews.

However, the public relations implications of SLAPPs may be more costly than the legal fees. Negative news coverage can damage organizations' reputation even further, especially if the public sympathizes with the experience of the contributor. Organizations can seem overly sensitive, not willing to take feedback, or appear hostile to customers. These attributes can further alienate potential customers and cause damage to the organization's reputation.

Gibson and Padilla reflect that SLAPPs are often appealing to organizations because they give the allusion of control.[18] However, they rarely benefit the organization's reputation and often result in hostile court and jury responses. Koprowski and Aron reflect that many judges are frustrated by SLAPPs and find them a drain on court resources.[19] Most SLAPPs are dismissed by judges and accrue many legal costs for both the plaintiff and defendants.[20]

SLAPPs and legitimate defamation lawsuits are a way that organizations attempt to use the legal system to regain control over messaging and digital reputation. However, they diminish the neoliberal public relations benefits from TPRS because they jeopardize the quality of information that comes from contributors. There are also concerns regarding the implications for open communication, dialogue, and free speech on TPRS.

Free Speech on TPRS

The key to the success and usefulness of TPRS is the ability for users to create content freely and that speech is protected, especially when it is opinion-based. The First Amendment to the U.S. Constitution states:

> Congress shall make no law respecting an establishment of religion, or prohibiting the free exercise thereof; or abridging the freedom of speech, or of the press; or the right of the people peaceably to assemble, and to petition the Government for a redress of grievances.[21]

Since its inception, countless lawsuits have tested the limits of the First Amendment, particularly the freedom of speech in digital environments.

While the First Amendment protects speech regarding government and public organizations, especially the right to levy criticism against such organizations, other legal rulings stipulate the boundaries of free speech regarding private businesses. Libel and slander cases can be traced to well before the U.S. Constitution – they were initially introduced as a means to remedy unfounded criticism against British churches.[22] The concept was carried over to the newly founded United States to help young businesses develop without fear of unfounded claims about allegiance and history.[23] As such, defamation lawsuits were used well until the twentieth century as a means to curb the creation and spread of unfounded messages.

It was not until the mid-1960s that the courts recognized free speech as excluding libel and slander, and even so, they have only ever applied the concept to public figures such as politicians. Lee adds, "The balancing of reputational and First Amendment interests, however, probably never will be fully settled."[24]

Reviews posted to TPRS are, in nature, opinions publicized on profiles of businesses. In general, the principles of free speech protect opinions, especially those that can provide evidence.[25] However, this raises the questions, "what is an opinion?" and "what differentiates it from fact?" In a 1990 case, the U.S. Supreme Court reflected,

> a statement is an opinion that merits protection when it is (1) about a matter of public concern, (2) expressed in a way that makes it hard to prove whether it is true or false, and (3) can't be reasonably interpreted to be a factual statement about someone.[26]

In these cases, a court would rule that the statement is an opinion and is not subject to a defamation lawsuit.

The protection of opinions as free speech and outside the scope of defamation suits covers most content on TPRS, although as organizations grapple for control of reputation, this protection seems weaker and weaker. As such, several defamation suits were recently appealed to the U.S. Supreme Court level, although the court has denied hearing any of them.[27]

Many suits have also challenged Yelp's responsibility for publishing libelous or defamatory reviews. As a foundation of digital policy of the twenty-first century, TPRS platforms (and other platforms) are not held responsible for the content published by users on their sites (this policy is not only reinforced through legal findings, but also through the terms and service agreements on most sites). Business owners who are upset with reviews but may be unable to challenge users directly because of anti-SLAPP suit protections in their state, have sued TPRS for their role in publishing libelous information. Again, none of these lawsuits were successful and the U.S. Supreme Court has refused to hear any of them.[28] In a 2019 case in California, where small business owner Hassell demanded Yelp pay damages for the negative reviews posted to his organization page, the court ruled that TPRS are not responsible for this content. A Yelp spokesperson reflected,

> We are happy to see the Supreme Court has ended Hassell's efforts to sidestep the law to compel Yelp to remove online reviews. This takes away a tool that could have been easily abused by litigants to obtain easy removal of entirely truthful consumer opinions.[29]

However, the publicity of these cases has significantly challenged the confidence reviewers have in posting reviews. For many reviewers, the fear and risk of being sued can outweigh the benefits of contributing to a review space. This jeopardizes the power of the review economy because it makes reviewers question the costs and benefits of contributing to TPRS. Without lawsuits, TPRS are spaces where there is relatively little risk, but many benefits for both contributors and readers. With the increasing presence of lawsuits and legal action against unfavorable reviewers, the cost and labor involved in contributing could be much higher. Defendants in site defamation cases must pay for legal counsel and invest time into proving their case.

When looking at news articles covering Polito's case, many other contributors have been faced with similar threats of lawsuits, thus deterring their willingness to contribute to TPRS:

> I wrote a bad review on the site of a computer company here in Winnipeg … About how he never installed a video card and how he never installed Windows 10 on my computer and my husband friend who owns part … of the computer company phoned him and told him that if I don't take down the post I will get sued.[30]

Many readers shared stories about threats from business owners after negative reviews, especially those that involved legal retaliation.

Other readers reflected that threats from businesses actually motivate them to further prove their case:

> I did have a real bad experience with an auto repair shop that missed major issues after an inspection i paid for, broke something that wasn't even related to the area they were doing work on, then tried to make me out to be the bad guy. The issue i am having is a legitimate problem with the business, so to me they are just empty threats and fueling more flame to the fire. When i am wronged, i won't just back down. This is of course from my perspective, and protected 1st amendment right. I would like to see this business try

and lawyer up, take it to court, fail miserably, then go bankrupt paying for the case.[31]

Here, the reader was motivated by the threats, and felt that the business would not actually have the resources to hire legal counsel and prove their case.

While many contributors take legal threat in strides, it is unclear the effect of defamation lawsuits on the public's willingness to labor over reviews. As found in the comments sections of articles on the topic, many contributors feared vengeful businesses and the costs of legally protecting themselves. However, others saw organizational threats of defamation suits as further evidence of the wrongdoings of that company, thus motivating further negative reviews. Without experimental research on this topic, it is unclear the impact of these actions (and the news media coverage) on willingness to review.

For reviewers worried about being sued, online blogs and journalists offer suggestions to protect their right to post content: "truth is an absolute defense for defamation. This means that if you write or state a review of a business or product, even if it isn't complimentary, but it recounts accurate occurrences, then you are likely not committing defamation."[32] Here, the reader suggests that even if an organization pursues a defamation suit, as long as a review is truthful, it should be protected. However, this would likely still incur the expenses of a defense attorney. So, readers provide other types of advice including (1) hedging reviews to denote opinions, (2) documenting threats, and (3) hiding identity when posting online.

First, readers recommend that contributors hedge their reviews by using language such as "in my opinion" or "I think." By doing so, the contributor clearly identifies their review as "opinion" which is widely protected from defamation suits that rely on the misrepresentation of facts, not opinions: "When you leave a review, always state 'in my opinion'. Don't leave definitive remarks either. You'll be fine."[33] Here, the reader suggests that by hedging a review as an opinion, businesses are less likely to retaliate or be successful at proving defamation. Importantly, this technique is not recommended by lawyers as a failproof way to prevent lawsuits or legal retaliation:

is it usually sufficient for a speaker to preface a statement (one that might otherwise be considered defamatory) with the words "I think" or "In my opinion"? The answer, of course, is no. People cannot say whatever they want and get protection for their comments by tacking on a couple of qualifying words.[34]

Second, readers identified the task of "documenting threats" from businesses to retaliate and protect contributors. Many readers viewed defamation suits as a risk for organizations, since suing a customer could have a potentially disastrous reputational impact:

> Go back, change your review to include that they sued you. They can't object to you saying something that is provable fact. I think a company suing reviews would be far more detrimental to them than a few bad reviews. Potential customers would realize they simply can't trust any of the positive comments posted.[35]

Here, the reader recommends that contributors document threats and all legal action so that it can be further publicized. As noted earlier, SLAPPs and defamation suits can do more harm to an organization's reputation than benefit, especially if negative news coverage conveys the business as in the wrong. Readers recommend that contributors use this as an advantage and publicize the efforts of any vengeful company.

Third, readers recommend that contributors hide their identity when writing reviews, that way organizations have a difficult time finding and proving who made the review: "I agree. I also don't leave reviews using my identifying information. A business would have to get a court order to have my ISP figure out who left the review, something ISPs resist."[36] It's worth noting that TPRS suggest that contributors provide factual information when building an online profile, but there are few ways that the platform can ensure this is done. For example, contributors could provide fake information and an alternate email address created just for reviews. This would make it difficult to identify the contributor and pursue legal action.

Some states have also developed legislation that would help protect contributors against SLAPPs and defamation cases. For example, California passed the "Yelp bill," which protects consumers who want to post a negative review about a California company. The bill penalized companies that issue SLAPPs or unfounded defamation lawsuits by assessing a fee for violating California policy.[37] Many individuals also have libel and slander coverage in their homeowner's insurance policies, which can pay for legal representation if a lawsuit is filed.[38]

Working Around the Law

Despite the growing number of lawsuits facing contributors to TPRS, the number of reviews on these sites continues to grow, demonstrating a willingness of contributors to accept the risks involved with posting. In addition to traditional reviews that reflect on the positive or negative experience of a customer, other types of content now regularly appear on TPRS, such as activist posts, reviews of individuals (not just businesses) and political discussions. These new uses and types of posts present a challenge for TPRS, organizations, and the legal system. The next chapter reviews how new posts work around the legal system and the traditional structures of TPRS to promote change in organizational, political, and everyday culture.

Notes

1 Cardona, C. (2017, August 4). "Bride, groom who slammed Dallas wedding photographer online, in media must pay $1.08M." *Dallas News.* Retrieved from: www.dallasnews.com/news/courts/2017/08/04/bride-groom-who-slammed-dallas-wedding-photographer-online-in-media-must-pay-1-08m/.

2 Shapiro, R. (2017, August 2). "Jury orders couple to pay $1 Million for defaming wedding photographer." *Huffington Post.* Retrieved from: www.huffpost.com/entry/jury-orders-couple-to-pay-1-million-for-publicly-shaming-wedding-photographer_n_59813d21e4b02b36343ecaea.

3 Cardona, C. (2017, August 4).

4 Ballard, J. (2017, August 2). "Wedding photographer wins $1.08 million in defamation lawsuit." *Resource Magazine.* Retrieved from: http://resourcemagonline.com/2017/08/wedding-photographer-wins-1-08-million-in-defamation-lawsuit/80039/.

5 Bernoff, J. (2017, August 1). "The Andrea Polito wedding photography lawsuit raises thorny questions about the groundswell." *Without Bullshit.* Retrieved from: https://withoutbullshit.com/blog/andrea-polito-wedding-photography-lawsuit-raises-thorny-questions-groundswell.

6 Cade, D. L. (2014, March 12). "Wedding photographers supposedly using fine print to sue clients over bad reviews." *Peta Pixel.* Retrieved from: https://petapixel.com/2014/03/21/wedding-photographers-supposedly-using-fine-print-sue-clients-bad-reviews/.

7 Cade, D. L. (2014, March 12).

8 Bernoff, J. (2017, August 1).

9 Hill, C. (2014, August 4). "You ruined my wedding – and you're suing me?" *Market Watch.* Retrieved from: www.marketwatch.com/story/you-just-gave-up-your-first-amendment-rights-2014-03-19.

10 Hill, C. (2014, August 4).

11 The Reeves Law Group. (2017). "Dallas wedding photographer wins $1.08 million against 'mean' couple who ruined her business." *The Reeves Law Group.* Retrieved from: www.robertreeveslaw.com/blog/wedding-photographer-defamation/; Walker et al. (1998, April 1). "WFAA-TV

Inc. v. John McLemore." *Supreme Court of Texas.* Retrieved from: https://scholar.google.com.tw/scholar_case?case=15201264378396618594&q=WFAA-TV,+Inc.+v.+McLemore,+978+S.W.2d+568,+571+(Tex.+1998).&hl=en&as_sdt=2006.

12 CBS News. (2019, July 22). "Posting a negative review online can get you sued." *CBS News.* Retrieved from: www.cbsnews.com/news/posting-a-negative-review-online-can-get-you-sued/.

13 CBS News. (2019, July 22).

14 CBS News. (2019, July 22).

15 Zhu, A. (2018, June 3).

16 Zhu, A. (2018, June 3).

17 Public Participation Project. (2020). "What is a SLAPP?" *Public Participation Project.* Retrieved from: https://anti-slapp.org/what-is-a-slapp.

18 Gibson, D., & Padilla, M. (1999). "Litigation public relations problems and limits." *Public Relations Review*, 25(2), 215–233. https://doi.org/10.1016/S0363-8111(99)80163–5.

19 Koprowski, W., & Aron, D. (2013). "Planning for the apes: Coping with guerrilla consumer behavior when the courts won't help." *Journal of Consumer Satisfaction, Dissatisfaction and Complaining Behavior*, 26, 110–120. Retrieved from: http://search.proquest.com/docview/1478021218/.

20 Sullum, J. (2009). "Slapp silly: Developers vs. free speech." *Reason*, 40(11).

21 U.S. Constitution, amendment I.

22 Lee, D. (2020). "Libel and slander." *The First Amendment Encyclopedia.* Retrieved from: www.mtsu.edu/first-amendment/article/997/libel-and-slander.

23 Lee, D. (2020).

24 Lee, D. (2020).

25 All Law. (2020). "Defamation of character or free speech?" *All Law.* Retrieved from: www.alllaw.com/articles/nolo/civil-litigation/defamation-character-free-speech.html.

26 All Law. (2020).

27 Robertson, A. (2019, January 22). "Supreme Court won't hear a lawsuit over defamatory Yelp reviews." *The Verge.* Retrieved from: www.theverge.com/2019/1/22/18193111/supreme-court-yelp-review-defamation-hassell-bird-section-230-lawsuit.

28 Robertson, A. (2019, January 22).

29 Robertson, A. (2019, January 22).

30 Freshbooks. (2020). "Can you sue over a bad review." *Freshbooks.* Retrieved from: www.freshbooks.com/blog/can-you-sue-over-a-bad-review.

31 Freshbooks. (2020).

32 Brenke, R. (2020). "Defamation in the age of Yelp." *Rachel Brenke.com.* Retrieved from: https://rachelbrenke.com/defamation-in-the-age-of-yelp/.

33 Komando, K. (2019, July 28). "You can be sued for posting a negative online review." *Fox News.* Retrieved from: www.foxnews.com/tech/you-can-be-sued-for-posting-a-negative-online-review.

34 All Law. (2020).
35 Komando, K. (2019, July 28).
36 Komando, K. (2019, July 28).
37 Bohgat, J. (2014, September 14). "California's 'Yelp' bill becomes law." *Above the Law*. Retrieved from: https://abovethelaw.com/2014/09/californias-yelp-bill-becomes-law/.
38 Bohgat, J. (2014, September 14).

6 Advocacy and Third-Party Review Sites

TPRS have become popular spaces for more than just consumer reviews of past purchases. Advocacy groups have turned to TPRS to share persuasive messaging and engage users to grow their following. In 2015, as Yelp continued to reflect on the issues that emerged from its scrubbing Dr. Walter Palmer's dentistry page after the hunt of Cecil the Lion, Yelp recommended users turn to "Yelp Talk." Hosted by Yelp, Yelp Talk is meant as a space for individuals to communicate and discuss current events, share opinions unrelated to a business or organization, and even engage in collective action. In short, Yelp encouraged those with activism goals to use the alternative site, thus separating reviews from activists.

Activism on TPRS seems to come from all political agendas. Consider the tale of two pizzerias. After the owner of Memories Pizza in Indiana vocalized his support of the state's "religious freedom law" (which gave power to business owners to invoke religion if the did not want to work with specific clients, such as same-sex couples), reviews from around the world turned to Yelp to shame the owner. Reviews such as, "I wanted some pizza after my klan rally so of course it was memories pizza," appeared on the site, and were quickly taken down by Yelp for violating the terms and service agreements. Users protested the conservative religious views of the owner of Memories Pizza, even at the risk of having their post removed by Yelp.

Alternatively, Big Apple Pizza in Florida similarly found itself the target of harassment after a photo of the owner picking up President Barack Obama in a bear-hug, went viral.[1] Users turned to Yelp to voice frustrations over the owner's embrace of the President, using the opportunity to critique President Obama's policies and stances. Again, Yelp removed the posts and encouraged users to turn to Yelp Talk, its online message board to debate and discuss current events and political opinions.

Protest posts that target specific businesses are more than just trolling, where users aim to elicit a response from others by saying extreme or hyperbolic things. There is evidence that TPRS can be spaces of collective action because contributors' function as cultural intermediaries that interpret organizations for public information. This chapter examines how activists have adopted features of TPRS and co-opted these spaces to use the power of cultural intermediaries and perform collective action.

Collective Action on TPRS

For many digital activist groups, the goal is to establish collective action, so that all members and supporters work together to achieve societal, cultural, or organizational changes.[2] Activist groups hold many types of goals from shaming dentists who engage in hunting, to marching for equal rights, to debating political issues in an effort to incur votes. In the past, these goals were achieved or pursued using traditional activist channels, such as face-to-face communication, televised events (i.e. protests, marches, debates), and advertising (i.e. commercials, billboards, celebrity endorsements). However, the popularization of TPRS provided a new channel that users could adopt and co-opt for persuasive purposes.

Rather than use TPRS in the traditional or normative way (where users provide reviews for organizations based on customer experience), activists co-opted organizational spaces to advocate for or against cultural issues. For example, after Ahmad Khan Rahami was identified as the suspect in New York City and New Jersey bombings in 2016, his parents' restaurant, First American Fried Chicken in Elizabeth, New Jersey became the center of political protests for anti-terrorism activists.[3] A deluge of one-star reviews with comments like "this chicken is the bomb" appeared on the Yelp page of his parents company. Within hours, Yelp added an "active clean up alert" pop-up window to the page, notifying users that the page was actively being scrubbed for activist content not related to the quality of the restaurant.[4]

The sudden appearance of thousands of negative Yelp postings was not coincidental, but rather a product of collective action taken by politically oriented groups seeking to generate awareness and cultivate support from the public. While the posts never last long (Yelp usually posts an active clean-up alert within a few hours of postings), the point is that the reviews were created in the first place, generating media coverage of their own. *Eater* contributor McKeever reflects, "these incidents prove how well Yelp has defined itself in the marketplace as the go-to spot for dining opinions. When someone perceives a restaurant as committing an injustice or being politically wrongheaded, Yelp is the natural flashlight."[5]

Collective action denotes that individuals must work together to maximize the impact and reach the largest audience. Yelp, seemingly, is a good place to both form collective identity and enact plans to carry out collective action. For users, activist groups can negotiate collective identity by identifying shared targets and negotiating the boundaries of membership (by dictating which behaviors are required). This can take place in both the traditional review sections of organization profiles or in auxiliary pages, such as Yelp Talk (discussed in the coming sections).

Either way, because of the controversial nature and topics of protest, in instances where collective action is enacted on Yelp, there is often pushback from both the platform and the targets. McKeever adds, "In these online protests, each side argues that the other is disinguous: The opposing side is often considered an out-of-control mob of bullies. But historically, these counter-accusations are characteristic of a protest, whether on social media or IRL."[6] Despite the newness of the digital Yelp platform, communication media have always grappled with integrating political speech and protest into organizational practices.

Cultural Intermediaries

Derived from Bourdieu's twentieth-century work on consumerism, cultural intermediaries refer to "those sets of occupations and workers involved in the production and circulation of symbolic goods and services in the context of an expanding cultural economy in postwar Western societies."[7] In this vein, cultural intermediaries interpret events and experiences and translate information to the public. Historically, cultural intermediaries referred to opinion leaders such as politicians, celebrities, and journalists.[8] For example, restaurant critics that shared reviews in newspapers held the power to shape how the public viewed a restaurant and its likelihood of success. These individuals could share their own experiences with a company, product, or service, therefore impacting how the public viewed that entity:

> They construct value, by framing how others – end consumers, as well as other market actors including other cultural intermediaries – engage with goods, affecting and effecting others' orientations towards those goods as legitimate – with "goods" understood to include material products as well as services, ideas and behaviours.[9]

Cultural intermediaries held power over the success of a product or service because of their social capital (trust from the public and resources to share information), therefore impacting public opinion.[10]

Since its conception, the category of cultural intermediaries was largely shaped by the technologies and communication channels available for information and opinion dissemination.[11] With the popularization of the Internet, the identity of cultural intermediaries was expanded to include reviewers on TPRS.[12] Like the traditional restaurant critics that published reviews in newspapers, now members of the public were welcome to share their interpretation. These reviews, as a collective set, impacted the public's orientation toward a company, service or product, therefore meeting the criteria of cultural intermediaries.

Importantly, Maguire and Matthews reflect that although the Internet and TPRS gave everyone the potential to serve as cultural intermediaries, the opening of the category to include any contributor has also challenged the power.[13] Because there are more reviews than ever before (and the number continues to grow), individual reviews and reviewers are less powerful than the traditional cultural intermediaries who were often singular voices dictating the orientation of the public. As a result, reviews are most powerful when they are read collectively, diminishing the power of one intermediary and celebrating the power of the collective.[14]

Programs like YES and upvoting on TPRS seemingly combat the diminished power of individuals by calling public attention to one or two reviews for each profile. In recognizing a few reviews, the platform reinforces those reviews as more powerful, thus reinforcing those contributors as cultural intermediaries.

Activists have also found ways to use the concept of cultural intermediaries to their advantage. By turning to other spaces on TPRS besides organizational profiles, they focus public attention to specific issues and events and take collective action to achieve goals. This includes spaces like Yelp Talk, which was designed by Yelp to give contributors a place outside organization profiles to reflect and debate current events and issues.

Yelp Talk

Yelp describes this section of its site as:

> a place for fun, open, and honest conversations about what's going on in your community. While it's easy to engage on Talk, take care with what you post – you can't go back and change your words later. A dash of common sense goes a long way.[15]

Major cities have their own Yelp Talk pages, so users are organized by either current or selected location. It functions mostly as a message board, where users can post content, and others can respond, without the possibility of deleting content later.

It is likely Yelp Talk developed to address the frequent use of reviews for advocates to shape digital reputation and messaging. Frustrated by this co-opting of TPRS, Google and Yelp both created alternative message boards designed to provide an outlet for individuals who want to communicate on a specific subject outside the boundaries of a normal review. While these spaces exist, it is also worth noting that activists continue to use TPRS to cultivate attention and persuade readers.

Regardless, Yelp Talk is a critical space for understanding how activists attempt to shape dialogue and perspectives on TPRS. By looking at online postings from individuals who self-identify as "activists," patterns of discursive approaches can be identified. This aids academic and practitioner understanding of (1) how activists co-opt TPRS to focus on specific issues, (2) how collective action is cultivated and used, and (3) how TPRS contributors serve as cultural intermediaries.

First, activists adopt several strategies when attempting to co-opt practices on TPRS and impact digital reputation. The term, co-opt, is used here to reference how activists adopt the practices of TPRS, but alter messages and intentions to fulfill their own goals. For example, when animal rights groups encouraged members to post on Dr. Palmer's dentistry page, the contributors adopted the standard practices of reviewing (such as providing a star rating, giving text-based information, and even pretending to be former patients. However, rather than providing truthful reflections on the practice, they used the space to criticize his hunting and draw attention to animal-rights groups, events, and initiatives.

When activists co-opt a space, they adopt the practices of the space, but have alternative purposes or intentions for their messages then traditional reviews. This is not to say that activism challenges the neoliberalism of TPRS – in contrary, it reinforces it. If the goal of contributors is to provide labor in exchange for information that may help or shape other customer experiences, activist groups seemingly reinforce this exact practice. Advocates exchange their labor for impacting others, particularly hoping to shape how users interact and support organizations. Like other contributors, activists share the same goals for their participation on TPRS.

On Yelp Talk, activists again engage this same pattern: sharing information (albeit persuasive messages) to change or impact reader opinions and future actions. Outside the scope of reviews, activists use Yelp Talk to re-direct user attention to selected issues or events.

For example, contributors asked users to sign petitions on hundreds of topics including: donating Michael Vick's salary to animal rescue groups; proposed laws on changes to mastectomy and breast cancer treatments; and advocates who want Joe Rogan to moderate the 2020 presidential debates. Users turned to Yelp Talk to vocalize support for an unlimited number of topics spanning political, cultural, and satirical purposes.

Second, spaces like Yelp Talk serve to discursively construct social movements and cultivate collective action. Like social media platforms such as Twitter, Yelp Talk encourages individuals with similar perspectives or opinions to meet and discuss critical issues and topics. In doing so, these individuals can form groups with specific intentions and goals. When these groups start to perform agreed and coordinated collective action, they become social movements, many of which then expand to other platforms or combine with efforts established on other platforms.

For example, the Black Lives Matter movement, which is largely established as starting on Twitter, was also a central feature of Yelp Talk's Chicago page.[16] Here, users debated the various goals of the group including reparations (emerging out of the 2020 Democratic Primary debates), investigations of police officers and departments, and general protest approaches (marches versus civil disobedience).[17]

Importantly, users turned to Yelp Talk not to just positively discuss the development of Black Lives Matter; there were many individuals who vocalized frustrations with the group and even challenged the evidence presented by supporters. There were even individuals who proposed conspiracy theories, such as Black Lives Matter protesters being paid $5,000 a month.[18] However, as noted by Edrington and Lee, users who vocalize opposition to growing social movements actually end up supporting it because they help define the boundaries of acceptable and unacceptable positions and therefore reinforce membership norms.[19]

Yelp Talk was also a space where collective actions were debated in the MeToo movement. For example, New Yorkers turned to Yelp Talk to share messages of harassment to shame the perpetrators and warn other women:

> Good thread. Whoever had this idea must be some sort of trend-setter. Now if guys are harassing you, rather than simply hitting "block", you can also say "if you ever contact me again in any format, I will post all of these pms on this thread (paste link)." I'm sure the creeps would be scared off at the thought of their creepiness being on public record.[20]

This type of action helped document and respond to harassment and abuse using the affordances of a TPRS where reviewing behavior and experiences was already the norm. Similarly, this type of collective action was also used on Twitter and Instagram as users shared experiences and expressed solidarity with other victims.

Again, like the Black Lives Matter movement, there were many users who vocalized their protest of the MeToo posts. However, these opponents served as an opportunity for the community to respond to criticism and further crystallize the boundaries of membership and the opinions of members. It is likely other activist groups use Yelp Talk to debate key issues, enact collective action, and establish the boundaries of membership.

Third, Yelp Talk provides a platform for cultural intermediaries, where individuals with social capital can interpret critical information and current events for readers. As Maguire and Matthews argue, TPRS turn members of the middle class into cultural intermediaries who serve "as market actors involved in the qualification of goods, mediating between economy and culture."[21] On Yelp Talk, this means not just interpreting organization and business quality, but also interpreting current events and controversial issues. For example, in the context of the 2020 U.S. Presidential election, contributors regularly shared their opinions on candidates and recent campaign announcements. While these interpretations were often debated by individuals with opposing perspectives, the initial post served as evidence of the labor involved in serving as a cultural intermediary.

Unlike the rest of the Yelp platform, where status of users is conveyed through the YES program, upvoting, and rating of posts, Yelp Talk does not have structural components that designate individuals as cultural intermediaries. Instead, this type of recognition must come from users who evaluate messages for status and trustworthiness. Previous work has demonstrated the ways that consumers evaluate messages in order to determine each of these credentials on TPRS, however, more work should specifically focus on spaces like Yelp Talk, where formalized markers are not present.[22]

Regardless, the labor of cultural intermediaries is present on Yelp Talk, even if the effect of this labor is unclear. As activists turn to message-board spaces on TPRS, they aim to interpret events and information in a way that furthers the commercial impact of some organizations over others. Posts are quick to vocalize support of organizations that align with activists' orientations, while calling for boycotts of others. During the 2020 Covid-19 pandemic, Yelp Talk was filled with calls for individuals to support some businesses that engaged in fair labor practices (such as paying employees during government-mandated shutdowns) and boycott others that laid off employees.[23]

Glassdoor Activism

Beyond the traditional TPRS spaces that advocacy groups use to promote perspectives and persuade the audience, groups turn to Glassdoor, an online database of organizations and reviews from former employees. Founded in 2007, the site promised to give potential employees a preview of working life by soliciting reviews from current and former employees at companies around the world.[24] Additionally, the site averages publicized salaries, pictures of offices, and contact information for companies.[25] By 2010, it started producing annual rankings, known as "the Employee Choice Awards," which recognized the best places to work in the world.[26]

To ensure that reviews actually come from current and former employees, Glassdoor verifies the use of organization email addresses and uses random screenings from content managers.[27] While most features are free to the public, paid subscribers can also access information, such as potential interview questions, provided by recently interviewed candidates.[28] Glassdoor also allows companies to post job openings and screen candidates on its site, a feature that continues to develop after it was acquired in 2018 by RecruitHoldings for $1.2 billion.[29] As of 2020, Glassdoor reported 67 million monthly users, which is ranked as the second largest job-site in the world after Indeed.com.[30]

Importantly, although Glassdoor aims to verify reviews and restrict reviews to current and former employees, the site has also served as a hub of activism. Various activist groups, especially those with political affiliations, have used Glassdoor to co-opt the information available on some organizations and cultivate social movements with political goals. This is particularly apparent when looking at the Glassdoor profiles of political groups such as U.S. Congress, the Federal Communications Commission, and even political figures like Vice President Joe Biden. Groups turn to these pages because they are considered an opportunity to impact the narrative of each organization, ultimately changing the perception and reputation of each entity. However, because of Glassdoor's verification processes, activists take a variety of approaches to adding content to Glassdoor, especially when contributors clearly lack the credentials (organization-affiliated email account) to post a review on a specific page.

The first way activist groups go around the required credentials is to partner with legitimate current or past employees. This is a common approach because disgruntled (current and former) employees may seek out partnerships that will enact revenge or share their frustrations with the public. In these cases, activist activities range from simply encouraging the review to fully drafting the review on behalf of the employee. For example, looking at the reviews of the Federal Communications Commission (FCC) illustrates many examples where users adopted advocacy perspectives in their negative reviews: "Seriously people – get a backbone and do your jobs. The bureaucracy is insane, and the lack of accountability is infuriating." Here, the contributor (a former FCC employee of five years), voices his frustrations and then criticizes management for the bureaucracy and accountability. These would likely sound like generic complaints about a former employer, except this language matches closely with the slogan of the activist group "Restore Internet Freedom."[31] Without confirmation directly from the contributor, it is unclear the role that the activist group played in the creation of this review, but the similarity in language reflects that there was either support or editorial assistance from the activist group.

Second, activists can pose as authentic current or former employees, post content, and accept when their posts are inevitably removed due to quality standards. Similar to the activist intentions of posts on Yelp, many activist contributors know there is a limited chance that their review will appear for more than one day at a time (and many are deleted even faster than that – if they appear at all). Despite the shortness of the life of an activist post, this is still a supported technique, especially when an organization is currently featured in news media. This means increased traffic to that organization's page, and a greater likelihood of it being viewed, even if it is just for a short period of time. This frequently happens when politicians (most who have organization pages on Glassdoor) announce their candidacy for national offices, such as President. For example, when Vice President Joe Biden announced he was running for President in 2019, his page was immediately filled by users claiming to be former employees, but mostly just airing grievances and posting messages of support or opposition to his past policies. While Glassdoor quickly removed these posts, their brief appearance during a time when more people would access this page reflected a type of political activism, even if it was short lived. It is likely for this reason that Glassdoor now employs an algorithm that monitors for extreme language and verifies the authenticity of user email addresses before reviews appear on the site.

And finally, former employees often turn into activists themselves, and join protest groups and engage in collective action. For individuals with political differences or grievances from their former employers, it is likely that after employment, they would join in efforts to enact change. This is visible when looking at the reviews of former employees in U.S. Congress. For example, some users reflected that they were frustrated over the lack of unions that represent the lower-level employees. They leave messages for future employees such as "Unionize!"

Within these three approaches to activism on Glassdoor, reviewers also act as cultural intermediaries who interpret the work culture and experience for potential employees and interested onlookers. Because of the verification process of each user, contributors are considered trustworthy and credible predictors of future experiences of the employer.

It is important to note that although activism is a growing part of all TPRS, there is limited research on its impact or the outcomes of such approaches. Activism on the sites usually garners additional media coverage, especially when an organization is already salient in the news. However, does this accomplish the goals of the group? How does it shape the opinions of onlookers and those who are targeted? More research is necessary before we can assess if these practices are successful (and in what circumstances) or fail to accomplish the goals of collective action.

TPRS with Activist Agendas

TPRS have also used their platforms to advocate for some political issues, particularly those that impact their operations. For example, during 2017, Yelp posted several articles and blog posts about upcoming FCC votes on network neutrality (aka net neutrality). The site encouraged users to vocalize support for network neutrality by signing petitions issued by Save the Internet, a non-profit activist organization that launched a digital crusade to demonstrate public support for the policy. In addition, Yelp changed its logo, briefly, to a page-loading symbol in order to cultivate attention for the issue. It worked, and users on Yelp Talk started a message thread titled, "Wondering what the Yelp logo is about today?" where dozens of users in each city shared information about network neutrality.

In a blog post that summarized Yelp's perspective on network neutrality, the company encouraged its millions of users to take part in Save the Internet's activist efforts:

> We want to keep the internet open and fair for everyone, which means ensuring that ISPs and other dominant platforms – like Google – prioritize consumers. Today, we're participating in the Day of Action to Save Net Neutrality on July 12. Please take a

moment to sign this petition, reach out to your Representatives and make your voice heard in support for net neutrality. At the end of the day, the internet belongs to billions of users around the world – not to a select few CEOs.[32]

Critically, Yelp sees its activist intentions as a differentiator from its main competitor, Google Reviews. Yelp criticizes Google for what it calls "anti-competitive practices in local search," or Google's rankings of local businesses when someone searches for a product or service category. Yelp argues:

Local search is one of the most important human behaviors on the internet. It is the bridge between online research and offline commerce. Local searches – people looking for a pediatrician in Munich, a hotel in Barcelona or a Thai restaurant in Copenhagen – comprise the largest single category of search, representing roughly one third of total desktop search volume, and over one half of smartphone search volume.[33]

Yelp, alternatively argues that its ratings system is dictated by user reviews, not on a hidden algorithm that prioritizes some businesses over others.

Considering the long history of fighting between Yelp and Google, it makes sense that Yelp would enthusiastically support network neutrality, especially in light of Google's wavering and seemingly inauthentic support of the same policy.[34] Acting as an activist for network neutrality by both supporting Save the Internet financially and by encouraging users to participate in its efforts, Yelp used activism to create parody with Google. And, despite the FCC voting to repeal network neutrality, it appears that Yelp's activism had a long-term impact on users, particularly those that supported this initiative. Threads on network neutrality appear frequently on Yelp Talk, and often refer back to the TPRS' blog post on the subject.

Both Yelp and Google Reviews adopted activist practices during the 2020 COVID-19 pandemic. Both sites created campaigns using their social media accounts to promote small businesses and (more specifically) continuing to purchase items like gift cards from small restaurants. Yelp also launched a $25 million fund to help struggling small businesses by providing micro-grants that would pay bills during forced shutdowns.[35] It also partnered with GoFundMe, the largest crowdsourcing platform in the world to integrate fundraising features directly on its site for independent businesses. Businesses that wanted to use this feature could opt for a "donate here" button to be added to their profile pages.

However, not all users agreed with Yelp's approach to activism during the pandemic, and some business owners turned to Yelp Talk to vocalize frustrations:

> I own Fireball Mountain laser tag and I learned from other laser tag owners that Yelp is responsible for setting up thousands of GoFundMe pages without the knowledge of the business owners involved. They are asking OUR customers to help them during this time by donating to GoFundMe. I as a business owner I never authorized them to do this or use my company to generate money for them both in the process. This is not only a scam, but I believe it is one of the more aggregious [sic] acts to assist them in lining their pockets using this horrible virus tragedy. Shame on both companies.[36]

The company later updated its post by saying Yelp was receptive to taking the "donate" button off its page upon request.

TPRS, like other organizations, must be careful about displays of authentic versus exploitive support and activism during crises.[37] Without critical user buy-in, messaging can be interpreted as taking advantage of national crises in order to benefit an organization's reputation. To address these potential problems, Google took a different approach to activism during the COVID-19 pandemic. Google partnered with the United Nations Foundation in support of WHO's global COVID-19 Solidarity Response Fund by matching donations ($2 donated from Google for every $1 from the public) up to $5 million. In total, Google committed to donate a total of $50 million to a variety of other services, including a distance-learning fund for students who need access to technology to complete schoolwork.[38]

As competitors in the review economy, Google and Yelp have turned to activism to engage users and establish parody. While Google has primarily used financial means to advocate for issues and responses to events, Yelp has turned to more traditional collective action techniques, such as information sharing, partnering with established activist groups, and calls for action such as signing a petition, protesting, and calling representatives. These practices more closely align with digital dialogic practices because they encourage dialogue between users and the organization (in this case, Yelp). While it is unclear if mutual adjustment is the goal of these initiatives, activism is a central part of each organization's plan to engage users and fully utilize the potential of neoliberal public relations.

Notes

1 McKeever, A. (2015, May 19). "Why Yelp emerged as a site for social protest." *Eater.* Retrieved from: www.eater.com/2015/5/19/8588185/yelp-protest-trolling-reviews-memories-pizza.
2 Tuomela, R. (2013). "Collective action." In *Encyclopedia of the Mind.* New York: Sage Reference.
3 Danovich, T. (2016, September 22). "What happens when Yelp restaurant reviews turn political?" *NPR.* Retrieved from: www.npr.org/sections/thesalt/2016/09/22/494935022/what-happens-when-yelp-restaurant-reviews-turn-political.
4 Danovich, T. (2016, September 22).
5 McKeever, A. (2015, May 19).
6 McKeever, A. (2015, May 19).
7 Southerton, D. (2017). "Cultural intermediaries." In *Encyclopedia of Consumer Culture.* Sage: New York. Retrieved from: https://sk.sagepub.com/reference/consumerculture/n147.xml.
8 Warren, G., & Dinnie, K. (2018). "Cultural intermediaries in place branding: Who are they and how do they construct legitimacy for their work and for themselves?" *Tourism Management,* 66, 302–314. https://doi.org/10.1016/j.tourman.2017.12.012.
9 Maguire, J., & Matthews, J. (2012). "Are we all cultural intermediaries now? An introduction to cultural intermediaries in context." *European Journal of Cultural Studies,* 15(5), 551–562. https://doi.org/10.1177/1367549412445762.
10 Wynn, J. (2012). "Guides through cultural work: A methodological framework for the study of cultural intermediaries." *Cultural Sociology,* 6(3), 336–350. https://doi.org/10.1177/1749975511401279.
11 Kobayashi, K., Jackson, S., & Sam, M. (2017). "Multiple dimensions of mediation within transnational advertising production: Cultural intermediaries as shapers of emerging cultural capital." *Consumption Markets Capital,* 21(2), 129–146. https://doi.org/10.1080/10253866.2017.1345421.
12 Benecke, D., Simpson, Z., Le Roux, S., Skinner, C., van Rensburg, N., Sibeko, J., … Meyer, J. (2017). "Cultural intermediaries and the circuit of culture: The Digital Ambassadors Project in Johannesburg, South Africa." *Public Relations Review,* 43(1), 26–34. https://doi.org/10.1016/j.pubrev.2016.10.009.
13 Maguire, J., & Matthews, J. (2012).
14 Moor, L. (2012). "Beyond cultural intermediaries? A socio-technical perspective on the market for social interventions." *European Journal of Cultural Studies,* 15(5), 563–580. https://doi.org/10.1177/1367549412445759.
15 Yelp. (2020). "How do I post on Yelp Talk?" *Yelp.* Retrieved from: www.yelp-support.com/article/How-do-I-post-on-Yelp-Talk?l=en_US.

16 Ince, J., Rojas, F., & Davis, C. (2017). "The social media response to Black Lives Matter: How Twitter users interact with Black Lives Matter through hashtag use." *Ethnic and Racial Studies*, 40(11), 1814–1830. https://doi.org/10.1080/01419870.2017.1334931.

17 O. B. (2016, March 17). "The Black Lives Matter Trump protest (one of a few)." *Yelp*. Retrieved from: www.yelp.com/topic/chicago-the-black-lives-matter-trump-protest-one-of-a-few.

18 O. B. (2016, March 17).

19 Edrington, C. L., & Lee, N. (2018). "Tweeting a social movement: Black Lives Matter and its use of Twitter to share information, build community, and promote action." *Journal of Public Interest Communications*, 2(2). https://doi.org/10.32473/jpic.v2.i2.p289.

20 A. A. (2014, November 29). "Thread where everyone posts any creepy or harassing PMs they have received." *Yelp*. Retrieved from: www.yelp.com/topic/new-york-thread-where-everyone-posts-any-creepy-or-harassing-pms-they-have-received.

21 Maguire, J., & Matthews, J. (2012).

22 Novak, A. N. (2016). "The revenge of Cecil the Lion: Credibility in online third-party review sites." In Folk, M., & Apostel, S. (Eds.) *Establishing and evaluating digital ethos and online credibility*. Hershey, PA: IGI Global.

23 B. A. (2020, March 15). "Restaurants open." *Yelp*. Retrieved from: www.yelp.com/topic/philadelphia-restaurants-open.

24 Wingfield, N. (2014, April 13). "The art of 'something from nothing.'" *The New York Times*. Retrieved from: www.nytimes.com/2014/04/14/technology/the-art-of-something-from-nothing.html.

25 Dishman, L. (2015, July 17). "What Glassdoor has learned from seven years of studying other companies." *Fast Company*. Retrieved from: www.fastcompany.com/3048590/what-glassdoor-has-learned-from-seven-years-of-studying-other-companies.

26 Grant, R. (2013, April 8) "Facebook voted world's best employer." *The Telegraph*. Retrieved from: www.telegraph.co.uk/technology/facebook/9978582/Facebook-voted-worlds-best-employer.html.

27 Wong, V. (2013, March 19). "Why employees like Zuckerberg (and other popular CEOs)." *Bloomberg*. Retrieved from: www.bloomberg.com/news/articles/2013-03-18/why-employees-like-zuckerberg-and-other-popular-ceos.

28 Balise, J. (2015, October 14). "16 unusual interview questions you may face at Facebook." *SF Gate*. Retrieved from: www.sfgate.com/business/article/16-unusual-interview-questions-you-may-face-at-6569103.php.

29 Musil, S. (2018, May 8). "Glassdoor to be acquired for $1.2B by Japanese HR company." *C-Net*. Retrieved from: www.cnet.com/news/glassdoor-to-be-acquired-for-1-2b-by-japanese-hr-company/#ftag=CAD590a51e.

30 Glassdoor (2020). "50+ HR and recruiting stats for 2020." *Glassdoor*. Retrieved from: www.glassdoor.com/employers/resources/hr-and-recruiting-stats/.

31 Rushe, D. (2015, February 26). "Net neutrality activists score landmark victory in fight to govern the internet." *The Guardian.* Retrieved from: www.theguardian.com/technology/2015/feb/26/net-neutrality-activists-landmark-victory-fcc.

32 Crenshaw, L. (2017, July 12). "Yelp stands up for net neutrality." *Yelp Blog.* Retrieved from: https://blog.yelp.com/2017/07/yelp-stands-net-neutrality.

33 Rossoglou, K. (2017, June 27). "How Google's local search results harm consumers and why the EU acted." *Yelp Blog.* Retrieved from: https://blog.yelp.com/2017/06/googles-local-search-results-harm-consumers-eu-acted.

34 Novak, A. N., & Sebastian, M. (2018). *Network neutrality and digital dialogic communication.* Routledge: New York.

35 Richard, C. (2020, March 24). "Yelp teams up with GoFundMe to make it easy for people to support the local businesses they love." *Yelp Blog.* Retrieved from: https://blog.yelp.com/2020/03/yelp-teams-up-with-gofundme-to-make-it-easy-for-people-to-support-the-local-businesses-they-love.

36 P. R. (2020, March 25). "Yelp and GoFundMe are running a Covid 19 scam!!! Shame on both companies for this sham!!!" *Yelp Blog.* Retrieved from: www.yelp.com/topic/wrightstown-yelp-and-gofundme-are-running-a-covid-19-scam-shame-on-both-companies-for-this-sham-2.

37 King, C., & Feltey, K. (1998). "The question of participation: Toward authentic public participation in public administration." *Public Administration Review*, 58(4), 317–326. https://doi.org/10.2307/977561.

38 PND Board. (2020, March 17). "Google commits $50 million for global COVID-19 responses." *Philanthropy News Digest.* Retrieved from: http://philanthropynewsdigest.org/news/google-commits-50-million-for-global-covid-19-response.

7 Best Practices

For contributors, businesses, brand managers, and even journalists, TPRS are an important, yet complicated space used to shape reputation and identity of organizations. As reputation is negotiated in this space, there is a set of best practices that helps all entities fully utilize the capacity of TPRS and achieve the neoliberal promises of the space.

Best practices are critical for TPRS' users because they establish a set of guidelines that help various groups achieve their goals. To develop best practices, the goals of each entity must be first articulated, so that the steps better meet these expectations. This chapter explores the goals and best practices suited to four groups: contributors, businesses, platform developers, and TPRS' users. It also examines how these goals may conflict with each group and how neoliberal public relations may help these groups work together.

Goals

As demonstrated in Chapter 3, contributors expect that TPRS allow users to regain control over the reputation and success of a business, product, or service. Contributors turn to TPRS to provide information to users and persuade users to support or oppose organizations before making a purchasing decision. For contributors, TPRS are an opportunity to also provide feedback to the organization, thus improving business functions and helping an organization meet the needs of the public. This is one reason why contributors are so upset when their content is "mismanaged" by TPRS through scrubbing; these unethical practices challenge how contributors can achieve their goals on the site.

However, for organizations, TPRS are new spaces to manage reputation and messaging that may reach a larger audience than current customers. Organizations pay attention to TPRS because they recognize the value of these platforms and the potential impact that posts can have on business success. It is for this reason that many organizations feel pressured into working with TPRS like Yelp to scrub away negative review and work with YES super-reviewers to modify the content of their pages.

TPRS and developers, like Yelp and Google Reviews, also have goals for the continued development and use of their platforms. As two of the first TPRS to make their sites profitable, increasing the amount of user attention and use of each site increases the amount managers can charge for advertising content, thus increasing revenue. As publicly traded companies, both are committed to increasing profits for shareholders, thus mandating that they continue to position themselves as appealing to potential advertisers. Based on the accusations of scrubbing, this means offering organizations more control over content in exchange for advertising purchases. It may also mean monetizing the data provided by users in the form of big datasets that can be purchased by other marketing companies seeking to create tailored campaigns to segmented audiences.

Finally, users of TPRS also aim to adopt the platforms to collect information before making a purchase decision. For users, TPRS are critical spaces where they can cut through the often-confusing messages of advertisers and marketers and get perspectives from other customers.

Because of the contradicting goals of these four groups, it is no wonder that they have grappled for control on TPRS over the past 20 years. TPRS began as a way for everyday consumers to regain control over organizations' reputation, and as organizations have attempted to take back that control, contributors and users have fought back. For example, when users were frustrated that their posts were being scrubbed away, they turned to Yelp Talk to voice those frustrations. And, when organizations were upset that Yelp asked for money to improve ratings, they sued. TPRS have also attempted to regain control by creating programs like YES, where user reviews are prioritized based on a history of credibility and trustworthiness.

These efforts largely indicate that there are expectations that come with the neoliberal labor dedicated to TPRS by all entities. Users expect that their labor will result in changes to organizational profiles and impact on the business practices and success of an organization (both for better and worse). Organizations expect that the labor given to managing TPRS will result in tangible changes to reputation, such as improved ratings and higher placement in search results (this is probably one of the reasons why small businesses sued and Yelp denied it ever promised better results in exchange for advertising revenue). Platform developers expect that their design choices and content impact the use of the site (such as the creation of the YES program). Users expect that, in exchange for their labor and attention given to the platform when searching for new organizations, they have access to credible and trustworthy information that will help inform purchasing decisions. In this vein, all entities have expectations for the exchange of labor performed on or toward these platforms.

Despite the problem that the expectation of each entity is seemingly at odds with the others, there are ways for each to maximize the labor performed on the site to reach their goals. The following sections recommend a set of best practices for each group to use to achieve the goals set forth by the expectations of neoliberal labor.

Best Practices – Contributors

Based on the observations from interviews with current contributors, organization managers, and users, there are four recommended best practices for contributors who aim to provide reviews that impact organizations and future (and potential) customers. First, contributors should aim to produce reviews that *emphasize specificity*. This means providing examples and giving specific recommendations for readers (both organizations and potential customers). Specificity can be demonstrated through using examples, giving context for experiences, and even providing quotes to support overall assessments. Reviews that provide specific details for readers are considered more trustworthy because they give additional context that can help a reader understand and assess the value of the information provided.[1] Organizations appreciate specificity because it tells them exactly what business practices people currently enjoy or what needs to be modified. Users appreciate specificity because it tells them exactly what to expect when engaging a business and what to avoid.

Second, contributors should *be transparent* about the context of their review and any factors that may impact their experience with an organization. One of the challenges of YES reviews is that many customers do not have the same type of interaction with an organization. So, while YES reviews appear at the top of any organizational profile, it is unlikely that the average customer will have the same type of experience. Although YES reviews are clearly marked, few YES reviews articulate the context of their interaction, especially in the cases where organizations have created specific experiences just for that reviewer. Being transparent in reviewing helps the audience determine the likelihood of that experience being replicated for them. Non-YES contributors should also emphasize transparency in their reviews. This means sharing any experience with the organization that may impact their experiences.

Third, contributors should *follow-up* on reviews to give additional information and revise earlier assessments, if necessary. In cases where a reviewer has had subsequent experiences with an organization, they have an obligation to update previous reviews with new information. This can help readers assess the consistency or the changes of an organization, therefore impacting their expectations. This means adjusting for both positive and negative changes in experience. If on a subsequent visit, the organization has improved on past problems, the contributor has an obligation to relay that improvement to users. Similarly, if an organization has new problems or the experience has changed for the worst, the contributor has an obligation to modify or update the previous review. When a contributor makes a review, they make a commitment that they will continue to relay information to the public, especially when previous assessments have changed. This does not mean the contributor needs to continually check back with the organization, but when presented with new information, they should relay it to users.

And finally, contributors should also *use TPRS* for information gathering for their own purchasing decisions. This not only helps the contributor identify aspects of reviews that are helpful or unhelpful (thus impacting the helpfulness of their own reviews), but it also helps fulfill the expectations of neoliberal labor. When contributors use the site for their own searches, they bolster the impact of other reviewers. When enough contributors adopt this practice, the impact of all reviews increases. Therefore, to make their own reviews impactful, they need to practice using the site when they intend to make a purchase decision.

Best Practices – Organizations

There are three best practices suited for organizations hoping to maximize the neoliberal potential of labor on TPRS to achieve their goals. First, organizations should use the information provided in reviews to *impact business practices*. When contributors provide labor in the form of a review, they give the organization valuable insight into the business practices that are and are not working for the consumer. Although there are many instances where reviews are more emotional than helpful, organizations should glean all possible information to help improve their business practices to better meet the needs of current and potential consumers. This means, at some points, taking painful steps to rectify the problems, such as modifying products, training staff, or adjusting customer communication. Organizations should recognize the value of the information provided on TPRS, rather than become defensive and diminish the motivations for the review or the contributor.

Second, organizations should adopt *digital dialogic communication* to achieve mutual adjustment. As identified in Chapter 4, digital dialogic communication employs the organization to seek out an information-gathering relationship with contributors in order to maximize the value of reviews. Organizations should seek out communication with contributors to gain more insight and meaning from reviews. By taking these reviews seriously and adjusting business practices, the organization appears more connected with customers, more dynamic in its ability to adjust to challenges, and willing to work with customers to give them a positive experience.

Third, organizations should *carefully consider* the reputational impact of lawsuits and legal action. Organizations considering suing for defamation should proceed cautiously; even when they have clear evidence that a review was designed to negatively impact reputation, the backlash from suing could be even worse than the initial offense. Organizations must also consider the SLAPP lawsuit policies of their state to ensure that they cannot be accused of suing to create a sense of fear. In cases where defamation is clearly present, organizations should work with legal representatives to exhaust all other methods before actioning a lawsuit. This means negotiation with the reviewer, attempting digital dialogic communication, and even working with the TPRS to eliminate the posts. Lawsuits, despite becoming increasingly common, should be a last resort.

Best Practices – Site Developers

TPRS developers must work to balance the needs of organizations, contributors, and general users. Each entity seeks to control the information on TPRS, but in the end, what information is displayed is ultimately at the discretion of the site developers and site managers (and the algorithms and editorial decisions they make). First, site developers should *emphasize transparency* in how and why posts appear on organization profiles and how they impact overall ratings. To eliminate concerns from contributors that their reviews are being scrubbed or censored from the platform, TPRS should explain clearly how reviews are ordered and where contributors can find their reviews. To address concerns from organizations that the platform unfairly ranks or orders reviews in order to benefit or harm the organization (based on the organization's financial relationship to the TPRS), site developers should explain clearly how reviews are ordered and what the algorithm looks for when ordering reviews. While Yelp already does both, Google Reviews is often criticized for its lack of transparency in review ordering, thus producing frustrations by both organizations and contributors.[2]

Second, TPRS developers should *avoid all unethical behavior* that directly or indirectly asks for money from organizations in exchange for improved ratings or rankings. Although TPRS like Yelp continue to deny that scrubbing ever took place on its site, lawsuits by small business owners suggest that, at some points, advertising sales representatives at least implied that a financial relationship between the TPRS and the organization would result in improved reviews and overall ratings. TPRS should avoid this type of language or vague promise at all costs, and actively work to eliminate any form of scrubbing on their platforms. Again, Yelp has clearly done this, but other platforms may not be as clear or take as firm a stance on the issue.

Third, TPRS should *monitor news and posts* for evidence that their platform is being used by activists rather than genuine reviewers. TPRS should also create separate spaces that give activists a place to voice concerns and engage in debate over contemporary issues. Because activist goals are often at odds with the credible and transparent goals of contributors and users, activist posts that attempt to persuade the audience without actual evidence or experience with an organization need to be removed. This does not mean deleting them forever, but instead moving them to a separate space specifically intended for debates and activism. Yelp developed Yelp Talk as an alternative, thereby giving the public a space to discuss relevant issues outside of organization profiles.

Similarly, TPRS should use *verification systems* to assess the credibility of posts and reviews. This may involve automated processes, such as looking at the history of reviews provided by a contributor (looking for consistency or inconsistency in the location of reviews), the history of upvoting of previous reviews, and the likelihood that a review is tied to media coverage or controversial events. This will help TPRS monitor for paid reviewers or activist contributors who challenge the credible nature of the platform. This should also include checks to ensure that the automated process is working correctly (by checking deleted or flagged content to prevent authentic reviews from being removed). TPRS should report back to accounts that are suspected of posting content that violates the terms and service agreements, such as activist posts or paid reviews. If done correctly, these measures should positively impact the credibility of the TPRS for both contributors and organizations.

Best Practices – Users

Finally, users or the audience of TPRS also have responsibilities when engaging the platforms. Because this category can also include contributors, organizational representatives, and TPRS developers, users must advocate for their own needs and demonstrate critical decision-making when considering posted reviews. First, users should *exercise caution and critical thinking* when trusting content on TPRS. As mentioned in Chapter 2, users seek out information from organization profiles, rather than specific posts. This means, looking at both positive and negative content, as well as looking past YES posts to other reviews. Users should consider a variety of factors, including: the number of reviews (profiles with more reviews are more credible than profiles with just one or two); the timeliness of reviews (users should consider that organizations have changed practices or offerings since older reviews were published); the credibility of the contributor (users should recognize the context of reviews, especially those authored by YES members or those that express a history with the organization); and the likelihood of organizational interference (does it seem likely that the organization paid for positive reviews or engaged in scrubbing?). Users are responsible for critically engaging content on TPRS and evaluating its usefulness. This may mean users should *verify information* by talking to trusted friends or family about their own experiences, looking for media or journalist reflections, or previewing the organization on other TPRS (including spaces like Yelp Talk). By seeking out this additional information, users can have more confidence in the information provided on TPRS before making a purchasing decision.

Users also have an *obligation to report* instances where they think unethical actions or unreliable information is provided. Although TPRS should employ automated algorithms to ensure the accuracy of posts, users remain the best way to identify problems for site intervention. Users must report suspicious activity to help other users avoid misinformation that may impact decision-making.

Additionally, users should return to TPRS after a consumer experience in order to *relay details* to other potential customers. This means users should post their own reviews that either confirm or challenge the information provided in previous posts. Because users benefited from the labor of contributors, they have a responsibility to return to the site and give their own labor to help future users. This fulfills the cycle of reviewing and ensures that TPRS continue to give credible insight into organizations.

These best practices for contributors, organizations, TPRS developers, and users suggest that all entities play a role in the credibility and usefulness of TPRS. When joining a site, each entity has a responsibility to ensure that the platform continues to be a helpful space for others, which reinforces its neoliberal role in the contemporary management of reputation and messaging.

Neoliberal Public Relations and the Review Economy

Neoliberal public relations practitioners assert that organizations should take advantage of the labor of contributors and users to adjust business practices to meet the needs and desires of the public. Neoliberal labor, like the type performed on TPRS, demonstrates the desire of the public to regain control over the reputation of an organization from traditional advertising and public relations efforts. However, rather than attempting to regain control, organizations can use the labor on these sites to fix their own business practices and achieve mutual adjustment.

The best practices described in the earlier section reflect ways that organizations can perform neoliberal public relations and use the neoliberal labor of the site. However, as noted in the introduction, organizations must recognize the role of TPRS and value the insights provided, rather than try to discredit posts that are unfavorable. This is easier said than done, and for many organizations, relies on the understanding of upper-level management. If organizations use the feedback of TPRS to modify business practices, TPRS can be a valuable space for garnering additional credibility and engaging potential customers (without organizational intervention). The autonomy of TPRS from organization control is exactly where the power of reviews comes from, thus actions by the organization that challenge this autonomy diminish the value of neoliberal public relations.

This, too, can impact the nature of the review economy where organization reputation is partially controlled by contributors and users instead of traditional public relations and advertising techniques. The review economy is predicated on the assumption that this control lies with the users and contributors, not organizational intervention. However, organizational actions like scrubbing or paying for reviews challenges the trust that users and contributors have in the review economy, thus diminishing its ability to also benefit organizations when reviews are credible and favorable. Thus, organizations should adopt the best practices outlined above to fully utilize, support, and benefit from the review economy.

Notes

1 Novak, A. N. (2016). "The revenge of Cecil the Lion: Credibility in online third-party review sites." In Folk, M., & Apostel, S. (Eds.) *Establishing and evaluating digital ethos and online credibility.* Hershey, PA: IGI Global.
2 Beaton, C. (2018, June 13). "Why you can't really trust negative online reviews." *The New York Times.* Retrieved from: www.nytimes.com/2018/06/13/smarter-living/trust-negative-product-reviews.html.

Conclusion

Contributors continue to labor on TPRS to benefit users and organizations and improve future customer experiences. As contributors perform labor, they silently hold expectations that other users are contributing information about organizations they may need in the future, therefore helping their own future experiences and decision-making. For contributors, this labor enacts a silent covenant with TPRS, namely that these online spaces will continue to function as a credible source of information when making purchasing decisions.

However, there are a variety of manipulations that occurs on (and off) these platforms, which voids this covenant. Many of these manipulations, such as paying for reviews, are hidden from the view of users, thereby making it unlikely that the public is aware of them. Others, such as scrubbing, are suspected, but unconfirmed, jeopardizing the trust between users and the platforms. Others still, such as SLAPP lawsuits and defamation cases, are widely publicized, impacting the security felt by contributors when sharing negative experiences. In short, the labor and likelihood of future contributions on these platforms is impacted by a variety of factors, many originating with organizations' desires to regain control over reputation on TPRS.

TPRS need to understand their own power within the review economy to better protect contributors and work with organizations. All entities stand to benefit from the labor performed on TPRS.

The Review Economy

Neoliberal labor is the key to the role of the review economy in the twenty-first-century marketing mix. As contributors perform labor to alter the reputation and messaging about organizations on TPRS, the power of these posts is challenged by the actions of organizations, the attention of users, and the design of the platform itself. Despite this, users continue to post and TPRS gain popularity as spaces for consumer research before making a purchasing decision. The power of neoliberal labor drives the trust and credibility in these platforms and continues to impact their popularity.

As TPRS continue to popularize and gain attention, they also continue to take power away from traditional advertising and public relations techniques designed to control reputation. As a result, organizations and users grapple for control in these digital spaces, often producing a confusing landscape of credibility, manipulation, and lawsuits. Despite the challenges of this negotiation, the economic prospects of organizations, services, and products continues to be shaped by TPRS and the information exchanged in these spaces. Three future predictions, and one future warning illustrate how the review economy will develop alongside the popularity of TPRS.

First, organizations that adopt best practices and learn to use information from TPRS will benefit the most. The nature of digital dialogic communication enhances organizations that commit to the work and labor required for mutual adjustment. Organizations that embrace the feedback in TPRS and use these spaces to develop relationships with consumers will benefit the most. This is not easy, especially as it means listening and responding to feedback that can be easy to discredit as emotional, biased, or uninformed. However, by engaging consumers in dialogue and using consumer feedback to enhance business practices and meet public demands, organizations can greatly benefit from these spaces.

Second, organizations will not stop seeking ways to manipulate the information on TPRS. As reviews become an even bigger impact on organizational success, it is likely that organizations will seek out new methods to impact these spaces. This will go beyond scrubbing and paying for reviews, and into other approved or subversive methods. While these behaviors are unknown, site developers need to manage these new attempts to impact these spaces to maintain credibility and transparency for users.

Third, users will demand more regulation and transparency with TPRS. Largely, TPRS remain an unregulated space, with limited state laws that guide the actions of contributors and organizations. Aside from anti-SLAPP lawsuit regulations in some states, there are no laws that regulate what information can be shared or eliminated on these sites. Besides the terms and conditions created by the site, there is no policy oversight that instructs TPRS on their responsibilities to users and organizations. Therefore, TPRS, organizations, and users develop their own standards and expectations, many of which are not met or enforced. As a result, users will eventually demand more regulations for TPRS to encourage transparency and credibility with online reviews. This likely means punishments for TPRS that accept advertising revenue in exchange for scrubbing. It is also likely that, as users voice demands of more transparency and regulation, organizations will turn to lobbying and political pressure to maintain their ability to impact these spaces. Ultimately, regulation is inevitable, especially as consumers demand more transparency and credibility on these platforms.

Finally, a warning to the conglomeration of these spaces. As Yelp and Google Reviews purchase smaller TPRS to maintain popularity and dominance in the industry, consumers should be cautious of how this impacts the credibility of these sites. With less site competition, users lose the ability to persuade platforms because there are limited other platforms for them to turn their attention to. Therefore, platforms have more ability to control the display of reviews, and organizations have more power to work with platforms to enact policies that benefit themselves. As in other industries, conglomeration means less competition, and less competition means less power to consumers. In an industry built on the promise of returning control and power to consumers, conglomeration threatens this prospect.

Next in TPRS

While Yelp and Google Reviews continue to dominate as the most used TPRS, newer sites promise users access to consumer and professional reviews in a variety of industries. Three TPRS illustrate how these sites may continue to develop, and what problems may lay ahead.

First, the mobile application Peeple was started in 2015 as a TPRS initially described as "Yelp for People."[1] The TPRS invited contributors to post reviews of people, rather than companies as do Yelp and Google Reviews, based on personal and professional relationships.[2] Critics warned that the application would cultivate a surveillance society where the public is encouraged to surveil each other.[3] Met with backlash, Peeple failed to launch and remains "coming soon" because of public outrage and concern that the application may contribute and cultivate a culture of cyberbullying.[4] Within a year, the application attempted to launch again, this time with safeguards for cyberbullying, but failed to gain enough public attention to justify the release of the application.[5] Critics noted that "Notorious people-rating app Peeple, the so-called 'Yelp for people,' has cut its most controversial features. There's no more reason to be afraid, but there's also no more reason to care."[6]

The failure of Peeple illustrates an important boundary of site use and purpose. Public and journalistic criticism of the application's early version, which allowed users to create profiles and review friends, family, and professional connections without their consent, demonstrates that there is a perceived difference in rating businesses and people. For users and other members of the public, businesses are fair game for reviews for two reasons, first there is a history of review culture stemming back to the industrial revolution and throughout the twentieth century. Second, businesses frequently ask for feedback in the form of customer-service surveys and market research. People, alternatively, do not request this type of feedback, especially in spaces where it is digitally archived and publicly available. Similarly, creating publicly available profiles (to anyone with access) without the consent of the individual also violates the privacy norms of the digital age. In short, Peeple failed, not because of the mechanism of reviewing, but because its subject was outside the norm of TPRS.

Second, Influenster is a website and mobile application that invites users to provide reviews of health and beauty products. Created in 2010 as a way for users to provide reviews of products frequently featured by influencers on social media, the site today boasts 4 million users monthly and encourages contributors and readers to vote for products that are the best within 99 categories (such as gel nail polish, vitamins, and moisturizers). According to developer Elizabeth Scherle,

> Influenster is the ultimate destination for consumers to get advice and learn about what's new and trending, curated from our community of socially-savvy beauty mavens. Through our peer-to-peer network of product discovery, over 2.5 million+ product junkies get to discover, review, and share their mutual love for products.[7]

Influenster's popularity stems from its ability to give users control over the reputation of beauty products that are typically touted by social media influencers. Like other TPRS, Influenster takes control away from traditional advertising techniques and instead gives it to consumers. Unlike other TPRS, Influenster focuses on product, not company, reviews, which developers argue help keep outside influence and organizational intervention out. However, organizations that do want to improve reviews can sign up to participate in VoxBox's, which sends free products to thousands of Influenster users to encourage them to review on the platform.

Finally, Trustpilot is a growing international site featuring over 70 million reviews of over 300,000 businesses around the world.[8] Instead of advertising, companies can pay for subscriptions to Trustpilot in order to access data about reviewers and additional details about customer experience.[9] Additionally, Trustpilot works with search engines such as Google to display positive reviews at the top of search results, which can impact the information a customer first sees when investigating a company before making a purchase decision. Importantly, Trustpilot gives organizations the power to curate their own review collection and share specific reviews with other sites (such as Facebook). Organizations willing to pay for a pro-subscription service (upwards of $599/month), have more control over review content and what information is visible to users.[10]

Unlike Influenster, Trustpilot aims to return some control back to the organization, despite its identification as a site. The site admits that when using a Trustpilot widget on your professional website, "you don't show consumers the full, accurate picture of all your customers' opinions."[11] Here, Trustpilot uses this to sell the pro-subscription service that allows organizations to manipulate the appearance of reviews, particularly on auxiliary spaces like the company website or on social media platforms.

Concluding Remarks

TPRS continue to grow in popularity and number of platforms. Within this growth, lies incredible potential to impact industries, organizations, and consumer experiences. By being mindful of the pitfalls of ethical and legal problems, TPRS can continue to secure contributor labor. Organizations can benefit from the feedback exhibited on these platforms. TPRS can grow profitable from advertising revenue. And, users can seek out information and opinions that will positively impact purchase decisions. In total, this labor produces a review economy, where the success of an organization is tied to its presence and digital reputation on TPRS.

Notes

1 Wattles, J. (2015, October 4). "Peeple co-founder pushes back against backlash over app." *CNN*. Retrieved from: https://money.cnn.com/2015/10/04/technology/peeple-app-social-suspended/.
2 Wattles, J. (2015, October 4).
3 Dewey, C. (2015, September 30). "Everyone you know will be able to rate you on the terrifying 'Yelp for people' – whether you want them to or not."

The Washington Post. Retrieved from: www.washingtonpost.com/news/the-intersect/wp/2015/09/30/everyone-you-know-will-be-able-to-rate-you-on-the-terrifying-yelp-for-people-whether-you-want-them-to-or-not/.

4 Pearson, J. (2015, October 26). "Peeple has backtracked to the point of pointlessness." *Vice.* Retrieved from: www.vice.com/en_us/article/vv74z3/peeple-has-backtracked-to-the-point-of-pointlessness.

5 Gollayan, C. (2016, March 7). " 'Yelp for people' app is back with safeguards for bullying." *The New York Post.* Retrieved from: https://nypost.com/2016/03/07/yelp-for-people-app-is-back-with-safeguards-for-bullying/.

6 Pearson, J. (2015, October 26).

7 Happi, A. (2016, December 19). "Positive influence." *Happi.com.* Retrieved from: www.happi.com/contents/view_online-exclusives/2016-12-19/positive-influence?123.

8 Alexa Data Analytics. (2020, March 31). "Trustpilot.com competitive analysis, marketing mix and traffic." *Alexa: An Amazon Company.* Retrieved from: www.alexa.com/siteinfo/trustpilot.com.

9 Trustpilot. (2020). "Why Trustpilot: Join the world's most powerful review platform." *Trustpilot.com.* Retrieved from: https://business.trustpilot.com/why-trustpilot.

10 Trustpilot. (2020).

11 WebArchive. (2020). "Add a TrustBox widget to a webpage." *WebArchive. org.* Retrieved from: https://web.archive.org/web/20200313095001/https://support.trustpilot.com/hc/en-us/articles/203840826-Add-a-TrustBox-widget-to-a-webpage.

Appendix
Methodological Notes

Chapter 2

This methodological approach prioritizes relationship building between researchers and interviewees to co-construct knowledge and meaning-making practices.[1] In-depth interviews are not limited to a closed set of standardized questions applied to all interactions, but rather built upon an agreed goal of identifying standard practices, attitudes, and discourses that define motivation and participation within a digital space.[2] In a study of public relations practitioners and their use of social media, Choi and Thoeni note that in-depth interviews make an ideal methodological approach for researchers attempting to unravel the relational complexities of twenty-first-century digital media management.[3] Duffy and Ney build upon this argument and note that while big data analysis has long dominated public relations, marketing, and advertising perspectives on digital organizational relationships, qualitative in-depth interviews provide needed nuance to statistical insight and conclusions.[4] This is especially true when studying motivational forces behind user engagement and digital consumer culture.[5]

For this study, 30 Yelp users were recruited through the Philadelphia Chapter of the Public Relations Society of America. Yelp users were defined as anyone who visited the site within the previous month to research an organization, group, or product. A set of 43 individuals volunteered, and 30 random individuals from the greater Philadelphia area (including Southern New Jersey, Philadelphia Suburbs, and Delaware) were selected for interviews. One-hour interviews were conducted during November 2019. Using a qualitative flexible format, the following questions were used to generate conversation about Yelp.

1. Informed Consent
   a. This interview is part of a series of interviews looking at how Yelp users create, read or use digital reviews. Your discussion will help researchers understand how Yelp users impact online reputation management.
   b. Statement of Anonymity

Opening Questions

1. When did you first start using Yelp?
2. What have you used Yelp recently to research?
3. Do you find Yelp a benefit or detriment to your research?
4. Are Yelp reviews trustworthy?
5. What would make Yelp more helpful to you?

Key Questions

1. Do you think business owners like or dislike Yelp? Why?
2. What makes a Yelp review helpful?
3. What do you think businesses can do to better use Yelp?

Closing

1. Thank you for your participation. The information you provided throughout today's discussion will be incredibly helpful as we study Yelp.
2. Is there any question I should have asked? (Prompt: anything else you would like to ask?)
3. Are there any questions I can answer about the study?

As per IRB recommendations, no data on participants can be provided in this publication. The following research procedure was used to translate interview data into findings:

Research Procedure

1. Recruit individuals for in-depth interviews. Randomly sample 30 participants from volunteers.
2. Email interviewees requesting a one-hour in-depth interview.
3. Schedule a time with each interested user.
4. Interview Yelp users individually using a schedule of questions.
5. Transcribe interviews.

6. Apply discursive analysis techniques to transcripts individually.
   a. Researchers independently read transcripts and apply Gee's identifying patterns of meaning-making, identity, negotiation, and terms of reference.
   b. Researchers independently generate list of discourses.
   c. Researchers meet to finalize list of discourses.
   d. Researchers re-read transcripts to look for examples of each discourse for findings.
7. Researchers present discourses to member-check participant for qualitative reliability.
8. Researchers incorporate response from member-check participant into findings.

Chapter 3

While previous studies have called for more qualitative insight into the motivations behind TPRS contributors and elite members, few studies have filled the void.[6] For example, Novak interviewed site users to study differences in credibility perception between standard reviews and those contributed by YES members.[7] Askay and Gossett studied YES members to explore the formation of digital communities using social network analysis.[8] However, beyond these two groups, few studies have examined or even mentioned YES within their framework. As mentioned previously, while limited attention to this topic exists academically, public relations practitioners demand more insight into this growing online group. This study examines how YES members identify themselves and explain their participation and motivation within the community.

To recruit YES members for this study, the researchers attended a YES happy hour in Boston, MA running concurrently with a large, international annual public relations conference. YES members were invited to a two-hour happy hour by conference organizers where they could network and mingle with public relations practitioners interested in learning more about the community, attracting YES attention for clients, or building relationships with YES members. In total, 44 YES members attended the event from 35 cities in the USA. A selection of 23 in-depth interviews was conducted with 23 YES members recruited from the event (and scheduled within the following week on-site in Boston). While all 44 members were asked to participate in the study, only 23 attendees actually responded and were willing to participate in the interview process. An anonymized description of each participant is included. IRB protocol limits the amount of identifying information included in this analysis; all participants were debriefed on the study and provided with an informed consent document based on university procedure.

Each interview lasted approximately one hour and was held in person or via Skype. Using Roca's qualitative reflexivity, each researcher began the interview with a set of predetermined questions, but was allowed to modify and expand questions as needed to fit new insights or areas of interest. This ensured that each interview was personalized and allowed for the discovery of new areas of interest or findings relevant to the study.[9] Recordings of each interview were transcribed and archived securely by both researchers. Using Roca and Karnieli-Miler, Strier, and Pessach's research methodology, the transcripts were analyzed using Gee's discursive analysis and Southwell et al.'s discursive approach to in-depth interviews.[10] The researchers read the transcripts, identifying patterns of meaning-making, identity, negotiation, and terms of reference.[11] For qualitative reliability purposes, quotes are used throughout the findings to support the analysis. In addition, a participant check was used. The final set of discourses and corresponding quotes was presented to a 24th YES member, who read through the paper and checked for the reliability of interpretation of each quote and finding.

Introductions

1. Informed Consent
   a. This interview is part of a series of interviews looking at how YES members engage in Yelp and digital reviews. Your discussion will help researchers understand how YES members view businesses and online reputation management.
   b. Statement of Anonymity

Opening Questions

1. How long have you been a YES member?
2. What inspired you to join Yelp?
3. Why did you apply for YES membership?
4. What are the biggest benefits for YES members?
5. What events or experiences did you enjoy the most as a YES member?

Table A.1 Participant Descriptions

ID Number	Location[1]	Age	Gender	Employment
1	Chicago, IL	24	Female	Flight Attendant
2	Los Angeles, CA	40	Male	Personal Trainer
3	Unknown	30	Female	Graduate Student
4	East Coast	29	Female	Elementary Teacher
5	Florida	34	Male	Business
6	Portland, OR	21	Female	Account Planner
7	Atlanta, GA	21	Female	Student
8	Pittsburgh, PA	30	Male	Insurance Company Employee
9	Washington, DC	31	Male	Political Consultant
10	Texas	29	Female	Software IT Developer
11	Pacific Northwest	22	Male	Unemployed
12	New Jersey	27	Male	Graduate Student
13	Hawaii	38	Male	Efficiency Supervisor
14	Northern Florida	39	Male	College Professor – Advertising
15	Boston, MA	21	Female	Student
16	Upstate New York	25	Female	Energy Company Employee
17	Midwest	28	Male	Sales
18	New England	38	Male	Science Teacher
19	San Francisco, CA	22	Male	Bartender
20	New Mexico	24	Female	Unemployed
21	West	25	Male	Unknown
22	Orlando, FL	22	Female	Retail Sales

1 Participants were asked for the region they associated with on Yelp. There were no limits to how they described this region, thus diversity in city, state, and regional identifiers.

Key Questions

1. How do you think other Yelp users perceive the credibility of your reviews?
2. What makes YES reviews more or less credible than other reviews?
3. What questions do you have for Yelp about the YES program?

Closing

1. Thank you for your participation. The information you provided throughout today's discussion will be incredibly helpful as we study YES membership.

2. Is there any question I should have asked? (Prompt: anything else you would like to ask?)
3. Are there any questions I can answer about the study?

Research Procedure

1. Attend YES Happy Hour and distribute contact information for follow-up in-depth interviews.
2. Email YES attendees requesting a one-hour in-depth interview.
3. Schedule a time with each interested party.
4. Interview YES members individually using schedule of questions.
5. Transcribe interviews.
6. Apply discursive analysis techniques to transcripts individually.

   a. Researchers independently read transcripts and apply Gee's identifying patterns of meaning-making, identity, negotiation, and terms of reference.
   b. Researchers independently generate list of discourses.
   c. Researchers meet to finalize list of discourses.
   d. Researchers re-read transcripts to look for examples of each discourse for findings.

7. Researchers present discourses to member-check participant for qualitative reliability.
8. Researchers incorporate response from member-check participant into findings.

Chapter 5

User comments on news articles are a valuable means of studying public reactions to developments in policy and current events. This chapter uses comments to illustrate public responses to defamation lawsuits levied against commenters on TPRS.

To collect articles for analysis, the 100 most popular articles on Google that referenced "Polito" or "Moldovan" were archived. Then, the researchers archived the comments section of each article for analysis. In total, 482 comments were issued on all news articles. Using Gee's meaning-making tasks, the researcher read all comments and identified discursive themes that emerged from the set of reader comments.[12] For reliability purposes examples and quotes from the comments are included in the chapter.

Chapter 6

To study how users turned to Yelp Talk and Glassdoor to discuss current events and activism, this chapter adopts a discourse analysis methodology adapted from Gee.[13] Similar to previous chapters, this methodology gives insight into the patterns of communication that emerge within a digital space, with special consideration of seven meaning-making tasks: significance, practices, identities, relationships, politics, connections, and sign systems/knowledge.

To collect data from Yelp Talk and Glassdoor, the researcher randomly sampled posts from pages of interest, including Yelp Talk San Francisco, Yelp Talk New York City, Glassdoor U.S. Congress, and Glassdoor FCC. By looking at posts over a long period of time, the researcher could identify patterns of advocacy as they appear on the platform. The chapter includes quotes from each page to illustrate how contributors attempt to co-opt the spaces for activist purposes.

Notes

1 DiCicco-Bloom, B., & Crabtree, B. F. (2006). "The qualitative research interview." *Medical Education*, 40(4), 314–321. doi:10.1111/j.1365-2929.2006.02418.x.

2 Choi, Y., & Thoeni, A. (2016). "Social media: Is this the new organizational stepchild?" *European Business Review*, 28(1), 21–38. doi:10.1108/EBR-05-2015-0048.

3 Choi, Y., & Thoeni, A. (2016).

4 Duffy, K., & Ney, J. (2015). "Exploring the divides among students, educators, and practitioners in the use of digital media as a pedagogical tool." *Journal of Marketing Education*, 37(2), 104–113. doi:10.1177/0273475315585826.

5 Roca, M. (2014). "Shifting to digital: Difficulties, challenges, and opportunities – A qualitative interview study of practitioners' experiences in the U.S." *Advertising & Society Review*, (15(3).

6 Choi, Y., & Thoeni, A. (2016); Karnieli-Miller, O., Strier, R., & Pessach, L. (2008, 2009). "Power relations in qualitative research." *Qualitative Health Research*, 19(2), 279–289. doi:10.1177/1049732308329306.

7 Novak, A. N. (2016). "The revenge of Cecil the Lion: Credibility in online third-party review sites." In Folk, M., & Apostel, S. (Eds.) *Establishing and evaluating digital ethos and online credibility*. Hershey, PA: IGI Global.

8 Askay, D. A., & Gossett, L. (2015). "Concealing communities within the crowd: Hiding organizational identities and brokering member identifications of the Yelp Elite Squad." *Management Communication Quarterly*, 29(4), 616–641. doi:10.1177/0893318915597301.

9 Jeong, J. (2011). "Practitioners' perceptions of their ethics in Korean global firms." *Public Relations Review*, 37(1), 99–102. doi:10.1016/j.pubrev.2010.09.004.

10 Roca, M. (2014); Karnieli-Miller, O. et al. (2008, 2009); Gee, J. P. (2011). *An introduction to discourse analysis: Theory and method* (3rd ed.). New York: Routledge; Southwell, B. G., Blake, S. H., & Torres, A. (2005). "Lessons on focus group methodology from a science television news project." *Technical Communication*, 52, 187–193.

11 Southwell, B. G. et al. (2005); Kyriakidou, M. (2015). "Media witnessing: Exploring the audience of distant suffering." *Media, Culture & Society*, 37(2), 215–231. https://doi.org/10.1177/0163443714557981.

12 Gee, J. P. (2011).

13 Gee, J. P. (2011).

Index

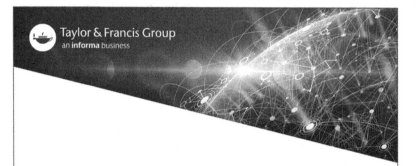

Printed in the United States
by Baker & Taylor Publisher Services